**Better Homes and Gardens**®

# fresh and simple™

# 5 o'clock grill

Better Homes and Gardens® Books

Des Moines, Iowa

**All of us at Better Homes and Gardens® Books** are dedicated to providing you with the information and ideas you need to create delicious foods. We welcome your comments and suggestions. Write to us at Better Homes and Gardens® Books, Cookbook Editorial Department, RW-240, 1716 Locust St., Des Moines, IA 50309-3023.

If you would like to order additional copies of any of our books, please check with your local bookstore.

 Our seal assures you that every recipe in *5 O'Clock Grill* has been tested in the Better Homes and Gardens® Test Kitchen. This means that each recipe is practical and reliable, and meets our high standards of taste appeal. We guarantee your satisfaction with this book for as long as you own it.

Pictured on front cover: Spicy Chicken and Star Fruit (see recipe, *page 15*)

Better Homes and Gardens® Books
An imprint of Meredith® Books

*Fresh and Simple*™ *5 O'Clock Grill*
Editor: Kristi M. Fuller
Contributing Editors: Carol Munson, Mary Willams, Spectrum Communication Services Inc.
Contributing Writer: Lisa Kingsley
Designer: Craig Hanken
Copy Editor: Marcia Gilmer
Proofreader: Sheila Mauck
Electronic Production Coordinator: Paula Forest
Editorial and Design Assistants: Judy Bailey, Jennifer Norris, Karen Schirm
Test Kitchen Director: Sharon Stilwell
Test Kitchen Product Supervisor: Marilyn Cornelius
Food Stylists: Dianna Nolin, Janet Pittman
Prop Stylist: Nancy Wall Hopkins
Photographer: Jim Krantz, Kritsada Panichgul
Production Director: Douglas M. Johnston
Production Manager: Pam Kvitne
Assistant Prepress Manager: Marjorie J. Schenkelberg

**Meredith® Books**
Editor in Chief: James D. Blume
Design Director: Matt Strelecki
Managing Editor: Gregory H. Kayko
Executive Food Editor: Lisa Holderness

Director, Sales & Marketing, Retail: Michael A. Peterson
Director, Sales & Marketing, Special Markets: Rita McMullen
Director, Sales & Marketing, Home & Garden Center Channel: Ray Wolf
Director, Operations: Valerie Wiese

Vice President, General Manager: Jamie L. Martin

*Better Homes and Gardens*® **Magazine**
Editor in Chief: Jean LemMon
Executive Food Editor: Nancy Byal

**Meredith Publishing Group**
President, Publishing Group: Christopher M. Little
Vice President, Consumer Marketing and Development: Hal Oringer

**Meredith Corporation**
Chairman and Chief Executive Officer: William T. Kerr

Chairman of the Executive Committee: E. T. Meredith III

# contents

# ah! fresh-air dining

During the week, a casual dinner with friends or a simple family meal doesn't have to turn into a major production. Grilling outdoors keeps preparation simple and cleanup minimal for the cook under time constraints. Better yet, it keeps the kitchen cool. The notable difference of *5 O'Clock Grill*, and all of the books in this series, is the use of fresh, innovative flavors created from easy-to-find produce and seasonings. Besides, what better way to unwind after working all day than cooking outdoors in the fresh air and enjoying a great meal?

# a passion
## for poultry

# chicken &
## prosciutto roll-ups

This pretty dish takes the Italian technique braciola—thin slices of meat wrapped around savories such as Italian ham, cheese, artichokes, spinach, and herbs—and applies it to chicken. Serve the attractive spirals with fresh spinach fettuccine.

**Prep: 25 minutes  Grill: 15 minutes**
**Makes 4 servings**

For sauce, in a small bowl combine wine and the 2 teaspoons fresh or ½ teaspoon dried thyme. Set aside.

Rinse chicken; pat dry. Place a chicken piece between 2 pieces of plastic wrap. Using the flat side of a meat mallet, pound the chicken lightly into a rectangle about ⅛ inch thick. Remove plastic wrap. Repeat with remaining chicken pieces.

Place a slice of prosciutto and one-fourth of the cheese on each chicken piece. Arrange one-fourth of the roasted peppers on cheese near bottom edge of chicken. Starting from bottom edge, roll up jelly-roll style; secure with wooden toothpicks. (At this point, chicken may be individually wrapped in plastic wrap and refrigerated up to 4 hours.)

Grill chicken on the rack of an uncovered grill directly over medium heat for 15 to 17 minutes or until chicken is tender and no longer pink, turning to cook evenly and brushing twice with sauce. If desired, garnish with additional fresh thyme.

Nutrition facts per serving: 214 cal., 9 g total fat (4 g sat. fat), 76 mg chol., 294 mg sodium, 2 g carbo., 0 g fiber, 27 g pro. Daily values: 14% vit. A, 85% vit. C, 7% calcium, 7% iron

¼ cup dry white wine

2 teaspoons snipped fresh thyme or ½ teaspoon dried thyme, crushed

4 medium skinless, boneless chicken breast halves (about 1 pound total)

4 thin slices prosciutto (about 1 ounce total), trimmed of fat

2 ounces fontina cheese, thinly sliced

½ of a 7-ounce jar roasted red sweet peppers, cut into thin strips (about ½ cup)

Fresh thyme (optional)

# chicken caribbean

Experience the islands without venturing off your landlocked patio. Fresh basil (try cinnamon basil if you can find it) infuses its aroma and peppery-clove flavor into the slightly sweet coconut-orange sauce—perfect with the spicy jerk-seasoned chicken.

8

4 medium skinless, boneless chicken breast halves (about 1 pound total)

½ teaspoon Jamaican jerk seasoning

½ cup canned coconut milk

¼ cup orange juice

2 tablespoons snipped fresh basil

1 teaspoon finely shredded orange peel (optional)

2 cups hot cooked rice

**Start to finish: 25 minutes**
**Makes 4 servings**

Rinse chicken; pat dry. Rub both sides of chicken with jerk seasoning. Grill chicken on the rack of an uncovered grill directly over medium heat 12 to 15 minutes or until chicken is no longer pink, turning once.

Meanwhile, for sauce, in a small saucepan combine coconut milk, orange juice, and 1 tablespoon of the basil. Bring to boiling; reduce heat. Simmer, uncovered, about 5 minutes or until reduced to ½ cup.

If desired, stir the orange peel into cooked rice. Serve chicken and sauce over rice. Sprinkle with the remaining basil.

Nutrition facts per serving: 287 cal., 9 g total fat (6 g sat. fat), 59 mg chol., 85 mg sodium, 25 g carbo., 0 g fiber, 24 g pro. Daily values: 2% vit. A, 13% vit. C, 2% calcium, 13% iron

## seasoned the right way

Marinades and rubs boost the flavor of grilled meats. Marinade, a liquid seasoned with herbs and spices, also can tenderize meat if it contains an acidic ingredient, such as lemon juice, yogurt, wine, or vinegar, or an enzyme found in papaya, ginger, pineapple, and figs. A rub is simply a blend of fresh or dried herbs or spices that's rubbed onto uncooked meats. For more rubs, marinades, and sauces, see pages 84 to 89.

# chicken with roquefort sauce

Roquefort—the king of French blues—is a sheep's milk cheese that, by law, must be aged at least two months in the limestone caves of Roquefort in the South of France. Serve this dish with some French bread, a crisp green salad, and a dry white wine.

**Prep: 12 minutes   Grill: 12 minutes**
**Makes 4 servings**

For sauce, in a small bowl combine yogurt, onion, Roquefort, chives, and white pepper. Cover and refrigerate until ready to serve. Brush the cut sides of pears with lemon juice. Set aside.

Rinse chicken; pat dry. Sprinkle with salt and pepper. Grill chicken on the rack of an uncovered grill directly over medium heat for 5 minutes. Turn chicken. Add pears to grill, cut sides down. Grill chicken and pears for 7 to 10 minutes or until chicken is tender and no longer pink. Serve chicken and pears with sauce.

Nutrition facts per serving: 199 cal., 5 g total fat (2 g sat. fat), 63 mg chol., 168 mg sodium, 14 g carbo., 2 g fiber, 25 g pro. Daily values: 2% vit. A, 9% vit. C, 8% calcium, 6% iron

½  cup plain fat-free yogurt

¼  cup chopped red onion

2  tablespoons crumbled Roquefort or other blue cheese

1  tablespoon snipped fresh chives

⅛  teaspoon white pepper

2  ripe small pears, halved lengthwise, cored, and stemmed

   Lemon juice

4  medium skinless, boneless chicken breast halves (about 1 pound total)

# raspberry chicken with plantains

**Plantains are a starchier, less-sweet cousin of the beloved banana. Unlike bananas, though, they must be cooked before eaten. Here they're sautéed in butter, a little brown sugar, and vinegar to make a delicious side to smoky-sweet raspberry chicken.**

1 cup fresh raspberries (½ pint) or one 10-ounce package frozen unsweetened raspberries

2 tablespoons granulated sugar

1 teaspoon margarine or butter

2 ripe plantains or firm bananas, sliced

2 tablespoons brown sugar

2 tablespoons white wine vinegar

2 green onions, thinly sliced

1 small fresh jalapeño pepper, seeded and finely chopped

4 medium skinless, boneless chicken breast halves (about 1 pound total)

Ti leaves (optional)

**Start to finish: 30 minutes**
**Makes 4 servings**

For sauce, in a small saucepan combine raspberries and granulated sugar. Heat over low heat about 3 minutes or until the berries are softened. Press berries through a fine-mesh sieve; discard seeds.

For plantains, in a large nonstick skillet heat margarine or butter over medium heat. Add the plantains, if using, and cook and stir about 2 minutes or until plantains are lightly browned and slightly softened. Stir in bananas (if using), brown sugar, and vinegar; heat through. Remove from heat; stir in green onions and jalapeño pepper.

Rinse chicken; pat dry. Sprinkle with salt and pepper. Grill chicken on the rack of an uncovered grill directly over medium heat for 12 to 15 minutes or until chicken is tender and no longer pink, turning once. If desired, place a chicken breast on a ti leaf; spoon sauce over chicken. Serve with plantains.

Nutrition facts per serving: 300 cal., 5 g total fat (1 g sat. fat), 59 mg chol., 103 mg sodium, 45 g carbo., 4 g fiber, 23 g pro. Daily values: 13% vit. A, 48% vit. C, 2% calcium, 11% iron

# northwest chicken salad

Perfect for an alfresco dinner on one of the first warm evenings of spring, this refreshing chicken salad features some of the season's best produce—crisp and tender greens, fresh asparagus, and sweet, juicy strawberries.

2 medium skinless, boneless chicken breast halves (about 8 ounces total)

1 recipe Raspberry Vinaigrette

8 to 10 asparagus spears

4 cups packaged shredded mixed salad greens

6 to 8 strawberries

1 pear, cored and sliced

2 tablespoons chopped sweet onion

8 to 10 pecan halves, toasted (optional)

**Prep: 15 minutes   Marinate: 10 minutes   Grill: 12 minutes**
**Makes 2 servings**

Rinse chicken; pat dry. Place chicken in a plastic bag set in a shallow dish. Prepare Raspberry Vinaigrette; reserve half for dressing. Pour remaining vinaigrette over chicken; close bag. Marinate at room temperature for 10 to 15 minutes, turning bag once.

Drain chicken; reserve marinade. Grill the chicken on the rack of an uncovered grill directly over medium heat for 12 to 15 minutes or until chicken is no longer pink, turning and brushing once with marinade halfway through cooking. Discard marinade. Meanwhile, in a covered skillet cook the asparagus in a small amount of boiling water for 6 to 8 minutes or until crisp-tender. Drain. To serve, divide greens between 2 plates. Slice chicken; arrange over greens. Top with asparagus, berries, pear, and onion. Serve with reserved vinaigrette and, if desired, pecans.

**Raspberry Vinaigrette:** In a screw-top jar combine $\frac{1}{4}$ cup pear nectar; 2 tablespoons salad oil; 2 tablespoons raspberry vinegar; 1 teaspoon Dijon-style mustard; 1 teaspoon toasted sesame oil; $\frac{1}{2}$ to 1 teaspoon dried basil, crushed; and $\frac{1}{8}$ teaspoon pepper. Cover and shake well.

Nutrition facts per serving: 379 cal., 20 g total fat (3 g sat. fat), 59 mg chol., 131 mg sodium, 28 g carbo., 6 g fiber, 25 g pro. Daily values: 9% vit. A, 85% vit. C, 5% calcium, 15% iron

# chicken & vegetable salad

**One of the best things about the grill is its inherent ease. Here, a colorful medley of vegetables is grilled in a foil-pack right alongside honey-mustard chicken. No pan to clean up, no mess, no fuss—and delicious grilled flavor to boot!**

**Prep: 20 minutes  Grill: 17 minutes**
**Makes 4 servings**

Fold a 48×18-inch piece of heavy foil in half to make a 24×18-inch rectangle. Place cauliflower, carrots, sweet pepper, and onion in center of foil. Pour ¼ cup of the dressing over vegetables; toss to coat. Bring up 2 opposite edges of foil; seal with a double fold. Fold remaining ends to completely enclose vegetables, leaving space for steam to build.

Grill vegetables on the rack of an uncovered grill directly over medium heat for 5 minutes. Meanwhile, rinse chicken; pat dry. Brush chicken with remaining dressing. Place chicken on grill rack next to vegetables. Grill for 12 to 15 minutes or until chicken is tender and no longer pink and vegetables are tender, turning chicken and vegetables once.

To serve, divide the greens and tomatoes among 4 plates. Diagonally cut chicken into slices; arrange on top of greens. Divide vegetables among plates. If desired, drizzle salads with additional dressing.

Nutrition facts per serving: 320 cal., 19 g total fat (3 g sat. fat), 64 mg chol., 342 mg sodium, 15 g carbo., 4 g fiber, 24 g pro. Daily values: 102% vit. A, 109% vit. C, 5% calcium, 14% iron

- 1  cup sliced cauliflower or broccoli flowerets
- 1  cup baby carrots
- 1  medium red and/or yellow sweet pepper, cut into strips
- 1  small red onion, thinly sliced and separated into rings
- ½  cup bottled honey-mustard salad dressing
- 4  medium skinless, boneless chicken breast halves (about 1 pound total)
- 6  cups packaged torn mixed salad greens
- 1½  cups cherry tomatoes, halved
  Honey-mustard dressing (optional)

# spicy chicken & star fruit

**It's a match made in heaven. The celestial star fruit (also called carambola) is a fitting addition to this chicken dish that's a little bit Italian (balsamic vinegar, olive oil, and rosemary) and a little bit Indian (cumin, coriander, and hot red pepper).**

**Prep: 15 minutes   Grill: 12 minutes**
**Makes 4 servings**

In a small bowl combine vinegar, olive oil, rosemary, cumin, coriander, black pepper, and red pepper. On eight 6-inch skewers alternately thread carambola and onions. Set aside.

Rinse chicken; pat dry. Grill the chicken on the rack of an uncovered grill directly over medium heat for 12 to 15 minutes or until chicken is tender and no longer pink, turning and brushing once with the vinegar mixture. Place kabobs on grill rack next to chicken the last 5 minutes of grilling, turning and brushing once with vinegar mixture.

Serve chicken and kabobs over rice. If desired, drizzle with preserves.

Nutrition facts per serving: 286 cal., 7 g total fat (1 g sat. fat), 59 mg chol., 57 mg sodium, 30 g carbo., 1 g fiber, 24 g pro. Daily values: 8% vit. A, 32% vit. C, 2% calcium, 17% iron

- 2 tablespoons balsamic vinegar or red wine vinegar
- 1 tablespoon olive oil
- ½ teaspoon dried rosemary, crushed
- ¼ teaspoon ground cumin
- ⅛ teaspoon ground coriander
- ⅛ teaspoon black pepper
  Dash ground red pepper
- 2 star fruit (carambola), sliced
- 8 green onions, cut into 2-inch pieces, and/or 4 small purple boiling onions, cut into wedges
- 4 medium skinless, boneless chicken breast halves (about 1 pound total)
- 2 cups hot cooked rice
- 2 tablespoons peach or apricot preserves, melted (optional)

# chicken with mango chutney

There are a variety of chutneys available on the market, but homemade is best—and who would have guessed something that seems so exotic could be so easy to make? This chutney features mangoes and is ready in less than 10 minutes.

- 1 ripe mango, seeded, peeled, and sliced
- ¼ cup dried currants or raisins
- ¼ cup thinly sliced green onions
- 2 to 3 tablespoons cider vinegar
- 2 tablespoons brown sugar
- ½ teaspoon mustard seed, crushed
- ⅛ teaspoon salt
- 1 pound skinless, boneless chicken thighs
- 1 teaspoon five-spice powder

**Start to finish: 25 minutes**
**Makes 4 servings**

In a medium saucepan combine half of the mango slices, the currants, green onions, vinegar, brown sugar, mustard seed, and salt. Bring to boiling; reduce heat. Simmer, covered, for 5 minutes. Remove from heat.

Meanwhile, chop the remaining mango slices; set aside. Rinse chicken; pat dry. Rub both sides of chicken with five-spice powder. Grill chicken on the rack of an uncovered grill directly over medium heat for 10 to 12 minutes or until chicken is tender and no longer pink, turning once.

To serve, stir the chopped mango into the cooked mango mixture. Serve with chicken.

Nutrition facts per serving: 205 cal., 6 g total fat (2 g sat. fat), 54 mg chol., 125 mg sodium, 22 g carbo., 2 g fiber, 17 g pro. Daily values: 22% vit. A, 26% vit. C, 3% calcium, 10% iron

# middle-eastern grilled chicken

The cucumber sauce served alongside this grilled chicken has nuances of tsatsiki, the yogurt, cucumber, and garlic sauce served at taverns on the Greek isles. Cucumbers are added to half of the spiced yogurt; the remaining half doubles as a brush-on.

**Prep: 12 minutes    Grill: 15 minutes**
**Makes 4 servings**

In a medium bowl combine yogurt, onion, oregano, garlic, sesame seed, cumin, turmeric (if desired), and salt. Transfer half of the yogurt mixture to a small bowl and stir in cucumber; cover and refrigerate until ready to serve. Set the remaining yogurt mixture aside.

Rinse chicken; pat dry. In a grill with a cover arrange preheated coals around a drip pan.* Test for medium heat above pan. Place chicken on grill rack over pan. Spoon the remaining yogurt mixture over chicken. Cover and grill for 15 to 18 minutes or until chicken is tender and no longer pink.

Serve chicken with the cucumber mixture and, if desired, couscous.

Nutrition facts per serving: 169 cal., 4 g total fat (1 g sat. fat), 60 mg chol., 166 mg sodium, 7 g carbo., 0 g fiber, 26 g pro. Daily values: 1% vit. A, 4% vit. C, 11% calcium, 9% iron

*Note: If using a gas grill, follow the manufacturer's directions for cooking by indirect heat (see tip box page 42 for explanation of indirect versus direct grilling).

- 1 **8-ounce carton plain fat-free yogurt**
- 1 **small onion, finely chopped**
- 1 **tablespoon snipped fresh oregano or savory or 1 teaspoon dried oregano or savory, crushed**
- 1½ **teaspoons bottled minced garlic**
- 1 **teaspoon sesame seed, toasted**
- ½ **teaspoon ground cumin**
- ¼ **teaspoon ground turmeric (optional)**
- ⅛ **teaspoon salt**
- 1 **small cucumber, seeded and chopped (about ⅔ cup)**
- 4 **medium skinless, boneless chicken breast halves (about 1 pound total)**

  **Hot cooked couscous (optional)**

# pineapple-rum turkey kabobs

Lemongrass—an essential ingredient in Indonesian and Thai cooking—imparts a woodsy, lemony flavor to the marinade for these kabobs. If you can't find fresh lemongrass at your grocery store, look for it at almost any Asian market.

18

12 ounces turkey breast tenderloin steaks or boneless turkey breast

⅓ cup unsweetened pineapple juice

3 tablespoons rum or unsweetened pineapple juice

1 tablespoon brown sugar

1 tablespoon finely chopped lemongrass or 2 teaspoons finely shredded lemon peel

1 tablespoon olive oil

1 medium red onion, cut into thin wedges

2 nectarines or 3 plums, pitted and cut into thick slices

1½ cups fresh or canned pineapple chunks

Hot cooked rice (optional)

**Prep: 15 minutes  Marinate: 4 hours  Grill: 12 minutes**
**Makes 4 servings**

Rinse turkey; pat dry. Cut into 1-inch cubes. Place turkey in a plastic bag set in a shallow dish. For marinade, combine the ⅓ cup pineapple juice, the rum, brown sugar, lemongrass, and oil. Pour over turkey; close bag. Marinate in refrigerator for 4 to 24 hours, turning bag occasionally.

Drain turkey, reserving marinade. In a small saucepan bring marinade to boiling. Remove from heat. On four 12-inch skewers alternately thread turkey and onion. Grill kabobs on the rack of an uncovered grill directly over medium heat for 12 to 14 minutes or until turkey is tender and no longer pink, turning once and brushing occasionally with marinade.

Meanwhile, on four 12-inch skewers alternately thread nectarines or plums and pineapple. Place on grill rack next to turkey kabobs the last 5 minutes of grilling, turning and brushing once with marinade. If desired, serve turkey and fruit kabobs with rice.

Nutrition facts per serving: 229 cal., 6 g total fat (1 g sat. fat), 37 mg chol., 36 mg sodium, 23 g carbo., 2 g fiber, 17 g pro. Daily values: 5% vit. A, 26% vit. C, 2% calcium, 8% iron

# five-spice chicken kabobs

**The Middle East goes Far East. Five-spice powder—an aromatic combination of ground spices that includes star anise, ginger, cinnamon, cloves, and Szechwan peppers—lends the Arab-invented kabob a Chinese flavor.**

¼ **cup frozen orange juice concentrate, thawed**

2 **tablespoons honey**

1 **tablespoon soy sauce**

¼ **teaspoon five-spice powder**

   **Dash ground ginger**

1 **pound skinless, boneless chicken breast halves or thighs**

1 **cup fresh pineapple chunks or one 8-ounce can pineapple chunks (juice pack), drained**

1 **medium green sweet pepper, cut into 1-inch pieces**

1 **medium red sweet pepper, cut into 1-inch pieces**

2 **cups hot cooked rice**

**Prep: 15 minutes   Grill: 12 minutes**
**Makes 6 servings**

For glaze, in a small bowl combine orange juice concentrate, honey, soy sauce, five-spice powder, and ginger. Set aside.

Rinse chicken; pat dry. Cut into 1-inch pieces. On six 12-inch skewers alternately thread chicken, pineapple, green pepper, and red pepper.

Grill kabobs on the rack of an uncovered grill directly over medium heat for 12 to 14 minutes or until chicken is tender and no longer pink, turning once and brushing once with glaze. Brush with any remaining glaze. Serve with rice.

Nutrition facts per serving: 218 cal., 2 g total fat (1 g sat. fat), 40 mg chol., 210 mg sodium, 32 g carbo., 1 g fiber, 17 g pro. Daily values: 17% vit. A, 132% vit. C, 2% calcium, 10% iron

## perfect rice, every time

Rice, a pretty plain-flavored grain, is a natural accompaniment to grilled meats because it soaks up the savory juices of the meat. For 3 cups (four ¾-cup servings) cooked long-grain white rice, measure 2 cups of water into a medium saucepan; bring it to a full boil. If desired, add ¼ teaspoon salt to water. Slowly add 1 cup rice, stir, and return to boiling. Simmer, covered, for 15 minutes. Remove from heat; let stand, covered, for 5 minutes.

# szechwan chicken strips

The longer you leave the chicken in its Szechwan-style (meaining spicy-hot!) marinade, the more intense flavor of chilies and garlic you'll get. Broccoli slaw mix and tomatoes make a refreshing and cooling accompaniment to the tongue-tingling chicken strips.

**Prep: 15 minutes  Marinate: 10 minutes  Grill: 10 minutes**
**Makes 4 servings**

Rinse chicken; pat dry. Cut into bite-size strips. Place the chicken in a plastic bag set in a shallow dish. For marinade, combine vinegar, hoisin sauce, Szechwan chili sauce, and garlic. Reserve half for dressing. Pour remaining marinade over chicken; close bag. Marinate in refrigerator at least 10 minutes or up to 2 hours, turning bag once.

Drain chicken, reserving marinade. On four 12-inch skewers thread chicken, accordion-style. Grill the kabobs on the rack of an uncovered grill directly over medium heat for 10 to 12 minutes or until chicken is tender and no longer pink, turning once and brushing twice with the marinade up to the last 5 minutes of grilling. Add the tomatoes to ends of skewers the last 2 to 3 minutes of grilling.

Serve kabobs over shredded broccoli. Drizzle with the dressing and sprinkle with peanuts.

Nutrition facts per serving: 205 cal., 4 g total fat (1 g sat. fat), 59 mg chol., 401 mg sodium, 16 g carbo., 2 g fiber, 23 g pro. Daily values: 8% vit. A, 51% vit. C, 2% calcium, 8% iron

- 1 **pound skinless, boneless chicken breast halves**
- ⅓ **cup rice vinegar**
- ¼ **cup hoisin sauce**
- 1 **to 2 teaspoons Szechwan chili sauce or ½ teaspoon crushed red pepper**
- ½ **teaspoon bottled minced garlic**
- 16 **cherry tomatoes**
- 2 **cups packaged shredded broccoli (broccoli slaw mix)**
- 1 **tablespoon chopped peanuts**

# turkey-peach salad

**Fresh fruit and poultry are a pleasing pair with a natural lightness. Here, juicy grilled turkey breast, peaches, and plums are artfully served in a hollowed-out peach "bowl" and drizzled with a light-as-air lemon-poppy seed dressing made with yogurt.**

4   **turkey breast tenderloin steaks (about 1 pound total)**

1   **teaspoon olive oil**

2   **peaches, pitted and cut up**

2   **plums, pitted and sliced**

2   **tablespoons lemon juice**

½   **cup lemon low-fat yogurt**

2   **tablespoons thinly sliced green onion**

¼   **teaspoon poppy seed**

  **Mixed salad greens**

**Start to finish: 30 minutes**
**Makes 4 servings**

Rinse turkey; pat dry. Rub both sides of turkey with oil. Sprinkle with salt and pepper. Grill turkey on the rack of an uncovered grill directly over medium heat for 12 to 15 minutes or until turkey is tender and no longer pink, turning once. Cut turkey into bite-size strips.

Meanwhile, in a medium bowl combine the peaches and plums. Add lemon juice; toss gently to coat. For dressing, in a small bowl combine yogurt, green onion, and poppy seed. If necessary, stir in 1 to 2 teaspoons additional lemon juice to reach drizzling consistency.

Divide greens among 4 dinner plates. (For peach bowls, see note below.) Arrange turkey and fruit on top of greens. Drizzle with dressing.

Nutrition facts per serving: 209 cal., 4 g total fat (1 g sat. fat), 51 mg chol., 96 mg sodium, 20 g carbo., 2 g fiber, 24 g pro. Daily values: 6% vit. A, 22% vit. C, 5% calcium, 7% iron

*Note: To serve the salad in peach bowls, cut 2 large peaches in half crosswise; remove pits. Using a spoon, scoop out some of the pulp to create shallow "bowls." Place on top of salad greens and spoon turkey and fruit into peach halves. Drizzle with dressing.*

# border grilled turkey salad

Try a fresh new twist on taco salad. Chili-and-lime-flavored strips of grilled turkey are served over crisp greens and drizzled with a hot pepper-spiced, dried-tomato vinaigrette. It's all topped off with crunchy crumbled tortilla chips.

24

4 turkey breast tenderloin steaks (about 1 pound total)

¼ cup lime juice

1 teaspoon chili powder

1 teaspoon bottled minced garlic

¾ cup bottled dried tomato vinaigrette*

1 medium fresh jalapeño pepper, seeded and finely chopped

4 cups packaged torn mixed salad greens

1 cup peeled, seeded, and chopped cucumber or peeled and chopped jicama

1 large tomato, coarsely chopped

8 baked tortilla chips, broken into bite-size pieces

**Prep: 15 minutes  Marinate: 30 minutes  Grill: 12 minutes**
**Makes 4 servings**

Rinse turkey; pat dry. Place turkey in a plastic bag set in a shallow dish. For marinade, combine lime juice, chili powder, and garlic. Pour over turkey; close bag. Marinate in refrigerator at least 30 minutes or up to 3 hours, turning bag occasionally.

Drain turkey, reserving marinade. Grill the turkey on the rack of an uncovered grill directly over medium heat for 12 to 15 minutes or until turkey is tender and no longer pink, turning once and brushing occasionally with marinade up to the last 5 minutes of grilling. Discard remaining marinade. Cut turkey into bite-size strips.

Meanwhile, for dressing, in a small bowl stir together tomato vinaigrette and jalapeño pepper. Combine greens, cucumber, and tomato; toss to mix. Divide greens mixture among 4 dinner plates; arrange turkey on top of greens. Drizzle with dressing and sprinkle with tortilla chips.

Nutrition facts per serving: 363 cal., 19 g total fat (3 g sat. fat), 79 mg chol., 402 mg sodium, 13 g carbo., 2 g fiber, 36 g pro. Daily values: 7% vit. A, 46% vit. C, 3% calcium, 14% iron

*Note: If you can't find dried tomato vinaigrette, substitute ⅔ cup bottled red wine vinaigrette and 2 tablespoons snipped, drained oil-packed dried tomatoes.*

# turkey steaks & vegetables

Vegetable juice—with a few added ingredients—doubles as a basting sauce for turkey steaks. Serve these savory grilled turkey steaks and grilled vegetables with chewy Italian bread and a glass of Chianti.

**Prep: 6 minutes   Grill: 12 minutes**
**Makes 4 servings**

For sauce, in a small bowl gradually stir vegetable juice into mayonnaise; stir in chives, thyme, and garlic. Set aside.

Rinse turkey; pat dry. Sprinkle with salt and pepper. Grill the turkey and halved zucchini and tomatoes, cut sides down, on the rack of an uncovered grill directly over medium heat for 6 minutes.

Turn turkey and vegetables; brush with sauce. Continue grilling for 6 to 9 minutes more or until turkey and zucchini are tender, turkey is no longer pink, and tomatoes are heated through,* brushing occasionally with sauce. Serve with any remaining sauce.

Nutrition facts per serving: 209 cal., 11 g total fat (2 g sat. fat), 56 mg chol., 200 mg sodium, 6 g carbo., 1 g fiber, 22 g pro. Daily values: 7% vit. A, 29% vit. C, 2% calcium, 11% iron

*Note: If the tomatoes are done before the turkey, remove the tomatoes from the grill and keep them warm.*

¼ cup vegetable juice

3 tablespoons mayonnaise or salad dressing

1 tablespoon snipped fresh chives or green onion tops

2 teaspoons snipped fresh thyme or ½ teaspoon dried thyme, crushed

½ teaspoon bottled minced garlic

4 turkey breast tenderloin steaks (about 1 pound total)

2 small zucchini, halved lengthwise

2 large roma tomatoes, halved lengthwise

# barbecued turkey tenderloins

**Southern barbecue goes gourmet! These substantial sandwiches feature spicy grilled turkey tucked into crusty French rolls with grilled tomatillos and fresh spinach. Try accompanying them with sweet potato chips, a tasty alternative to regular chips.**

**Prep: 10 minutes   Grill: 20 minutes**
**Makes 4 servings**

For sauce, in a small bowl combine barbecue sauce, jalapeño pepper, and tahini. Transfer half of the sauce to another bowl for basting. Reserve remaining sauce until ready to serve. On two 8- to 10-inch skewers thread tomatillos, if using. Set aside.

Rinse turkey; pat dry. Brush both sides of turkey with basting sauce. Grill turkey on the greased rack of an uncovered grill directly over medium heat about 20 minutes or until the turkey is tender and no longer pink, turning and brushing once with basting sauce. Place tomatillos on the grill rack next to the turkey the last 8 minutes of grilling or until tender, turning once. Thinly slice turkey and chop tomatillos.

Toast the rolls on the grill. To serve, fill the rolls with a few spinach leaves, the grilled turkey, and tomatillos or salsa verde. Spoon on the reserved sauce.

Nutrition facts per serving: 378 cal., 8 g total fat (2 g sat. fat), 50 mg chol., 776 mg sodium, 45 g carbo., 1 g fiber, 30 g pro. Daily values: 12% vit. A, 24% vit. C, 9% calcium, 25% iron

*\*Note: Tahini is a thick paste that is made by crushing sesame seeds. It it most often used in Middle Eastern dishes and can be found in the ethnic foods section of most supermarkets.*

½ **cup bottled onion-hickory barbecue sauce**

1 **small fresh jalapeño pepper, seeded and finely chopped**

1 **tablespoon tahini (sesame butter)\***

4 **tomatillos, husked and halved lengthwise, or ½ cup salsa verde**

2 **turkey breast tenderloins (about 1 pound total)**

4 **French-style rolls, split**

**Spinach leaves**

beef it up

# garlic steaks with nectarine-onion relish

**What's better than the smell of steak on the grill in the summertime? The aroma of garlic-studded beef on the grill. The mint-scented relish features one of summer's favorite fruits. Serve this steak with some crusty bread to soak up the delicious juices.**

**Prep: 25 minutes   Grill: 8 minutes**
**Makes 4 servings**

Trim fat from steaks. With the point of a paring knife, make small slits in steaks. Insert half of the garlic into slits. Wrap steaks in plastic wrap; let stand at room temperature up to 20 minutes. (For more intense flavor, refrigerate up to 8 hours.) Sprinkle with salt and pepper.

Meanwhile, for relish, in a large nonstick skillet cook onions and remaining garlic in hot oil over medium heat about 10 minutes or until onions are a deep golden color (but not brown), stirring occasionally. Stir in vinegar and honey. Stir in nectarine and the 2 teaspoons mint; heat through.

Grill steaks on the rack of an uncovered grill directly over medium heat to desired doneness, turning once. (Allow 8 to 12 minutes for medium-rare and 12 to 15 minutes for medium doneness.) Serve the relish with steaks. If desired, garnish with additional mint.

Nutrition facts per serving: 272 cal., 9 g total fat (3 g sat. fat), 97 mg chol., 108 mg sodium, 13 g carbo., 1 g fiber, 34 g pro. Daily values: 2% vit. A, 9% vit. C, 2% calcium, 27% iron

- 4 **boneless beef top loin steaks, cut 1 inch thick (about 1½ to 2 pounds total)**
- 6 **cloves garlic, thinly sliced**
- 2 **medium onions, coarsely chopped**
- 1 **teaspoon olive oil**
- 2 **tablespoons cider vinegar**
- 1 **tablespoon honey**
- 1 **medium nectarine, chopped**
- 2 **teaspoons snipped fresh applemint, pineapplemint, or spearmint**

  **Fresh applemint, pineapplemint, or spearmint (optional)**

# rosemary beef with sweet pepper relish

**The head-clearing tang of horseradish and the mellow-but-hearty flavor of beef go well together. Here, they're even better joined with a rub of fresh rosemary, garlic, and olive oil. An onion-and-pepper relish conveniently cooks in a foil-pack along with the steaks.**

1 medium onion, thinly sliced

1 red or yellow sweet pepper, cut into strips

1 tablespoon red wine vinegar

1 tablespoon olive oil

⅛ teaspoon black pepper

2 teaspoons snipped fresh rosemary

2 teaspoons bottled minced garlic

4 boneless beef top loin steaks, cut 1 inch thick (about 1 pound total)

1 tablespoon prepared horseradish

**Prep: 15 minutes   Grill: 8 minutes**
**Makes 4 servings**

For relish, fold a 24×18-inch piece of heavy foil in half to make a 12×18-inch rectangle. Place onion and sweet pepper in center of foil. Drizzle vinegar and 2 teaspoons of the oil over vegetables; sprinkle with black pepper. Bring up 2 opposite edges of foil; seal with a double fold. Fold remaining ends to completely enclose vegetables, leaving space for steam to build. Set aside.

In a small bowl combine the remaining oil, the rosemary, and garlic. Trim fat from steaks. Rub steaks with rosemary mixture. Spread one side of the steaks with horseradish.

Grill steaks and relish on the rack of an uncovered grill directly over medium heat until steaks are cooked to desired doneness, turning steaks and relish once. (Allow 8 to 12 minutes for medium-rare and 12 to 15 minutes for medium doneness.) Spoon the relish over steaks.

Nutrition facts per serving: 198 cal., 9 g total fat (2 g sat. fat), 65 mg chol., 92 mg sodium, 7 g carbo., 1 g fiber, 23 g pro. Daily values: 13% vit. A, 58% vit. C, 2% calcium, 19% iron

# filet mignon with portobello sauce

Just a splash of Madeira or port wine makes this buttery, meltingly tender steak-and-mushroom dish simply marvelous. Madeira and port are both slightly sweet Spanish wines flavored with a bit of brandy.

**Prep: 15 minutes    Grill: 8 minutes**
**Makes 4 servings**

Trim fat from steaks. Rub both sides of steaks with oil and pepper. Grill steaks on the rack of an uncovered grill directly over medium heat to desired doneness, turning once. (Allow 8 to 12 minutes for medium-rare and 12 to 15 minutes for medium doneness.)

Meanwhile, for sauce, in a large skillet cook and stir mushrooms and onions in hot margarine over medium heat about 5 minutes or until vegetables are tender. Stir in broth and Madeira or port. Bring to boiling. Remove from heat. Thinly slice steaks diagonally and serve with sauce.

Nutrition facts per serving: 260 cal., 13 g total fat (4 g sat. fat), 80 mg chol., 160 mg sodium, 4 g carbo., 1 g fiber, 29 g pro. Daily values: 8% vit. A, 11% vit. C, 1% calcium, 31% iron

- 4 beef tenderloin steaks, cut 1 inch thick (about 1¼ pounds total)
- 1 teaspoon olive oil
- ¼ teaspoon pepper
- 2 large portobello mushrooms, halved and sliced
- 8 green onions, cut into 1-inch pieces
- 1 tablespoon margarine or butter
- ⅓ cup beef broth
- 2 tablespoons Madeira or port wine

### ready, set, grill!
The cooking times in this book don't include time to heat up the coals in a standard grill—but you won't lose any time if you light the coals first so they can be heating while you're preparing the food. Traditional briquettes—once lit—take about 20 to 30 minutes to burn hot enough for cooking. They should be ash-gray in daylight or glowing red all over in darkness. Convenient self-lighting coals need just 5 to 10 minutes before they're ready to go. If you have a gas grill, check your owner's manual for times.

# beef & fruit salad

For an exotic presentation, serve the fruit mixture in a kiwano (kee-WAH-noh) shell. Also called "horned melon," the kiwano has a jellylike pulp with a tart, yet sweet flavor likened to a combination of banana and cucumber.

**Prep: 20 minutes    Marinate: 30 minutes    Grill: 8 minutes
Makes 4 servings**

Trim fat from steak. Place steak in a plastic bag set in a shallow dish. For marinade, combine the teriyaki sauce, lemon juice, water, oil, and hot pepper sauce. Reserve ⅓ cup for dressing. Pour remaining marinade over steak; close bag. Marinate at room temperature up to 30 minutes, turning bag occasionally. (Or, marinate in refrigerator up to 8 hours.)

Drain steak, reserving marinade. Grill steak on the rack of an uncovered grill directly over medium heat to desired doneness, turning once and brushing occasionally with marinade up to the last 5 minutes of grilling. (Allow 8 to 12 minutes for medium-rare doneness and 12 to 15 minutes for medium doneness.) Discard any remaining marinade.

To serve, divide cabbage and sorrel among 4 dinner plates. Thinly slice steak diagonally. Arrange steak and fruit on top of greens. Drizzle with the dressing (and, if desired, pulp of kiwano fruit). If desired, serve fruit in kiwano shells.*

Nutrition facts per serving: 248 cal., 10 g total fat (3 g sat. fat), 57 mg chol., 307 mg sodium, 19 g carbo., 2 g fiber, 22 g pro. Daily values: 19% vit. A, 86% vit. C, 6% calcium, 19% iron

*Note: To serve in kiwano shells, cut each kiwano in half crosswise. Scoop out pulp.

- 12 ounces boneless beef sirloin steak, cut 1 inch thick
- ⅓ cup reduced-sodium teriyaki sauce or soy sauce
- ¼ cup lemon juice
- ¼ cup water
- 2 teaspoons toasted sesame oil
- ⅛ teaspoon bottled hot pepper sauce
- 3 cups shredded napa cabbage
- 1 cup torn or shredded sorrel or spinach
- 2 cups fresh fruit (choose from sliced plums, nectarines, or kiwifruit; halved seedless grapes or strawberries; raspberries; and/or blueberries)
- 2 kiwanos (optional)

# beef & avocado tacos

Try the real flavors of Mexico with these soft tacos filled with grilled sirloin, peppers, and onions. True caballeros enjoy their tacos and burritos made with carne asada, or "grilled meat," and a little picante sauce.

2 tablespoons lemon juice

1 avocado, seeded, peeled, and cut into ½-inch cubes

1 pound boneless beef sirloin or eye round steak, cut 1 inch thick

1 medium onion, cut into wedges

2 fresh cubanelle, Anaheim, or poblano peppers, cut into 1-inch squares

1 tablespoon olive oil

½ cup picante sauce

2 cups shredded lettuce

4 7- to 8-inch flour tortillas

**Prep: 20 minutes   Grill: 10 minutes**
**Makes 4 servings**

Drizzle lemon juice over avocado; toss gently to coat. Set aside.

Trim fat from steak. Cut steak into 2×1-inch thin strips. On four 12-inch skewers thread steak, accordion-style. On four 12-inch skewers alternately thread onion and peppers. Brush vegetables with oil.

Grill the kabobs on the rack of an uncovered grill directly over medium heat for 10 to 12 minutes or until steak is cooked to desired doneness, turning kabobs once and brushing occasionally with picante sauce.

To serve, divide the steak, onion, peppers, avocado, and lettuce among the tortillas. Fold tortillas over filling. If desired, serve with additional picante sauce.

Nutrition facts per serving: 425 cal., 24 g total fat (6 g sat. fat), 76 mg chol., 403 mg sodium, 24 g carbo., 3 g fiber, 30 g pro. Daily values: 7% vit. A, 105% vit. C, 5% calcium, 32% iron

# jalapeño beef kabobs

Firecracker-hot but as sweet-as-pie, jalapeño pepper jelly adds tongue-tingling zing to these beef kabobs. Baby pattypan squash and tomatillos, with their green-tomato texture and lemon-apple essence, add even more interest.

**Prep: 15 minutes    Grill: 12 minutes**
**Makes 4 servings**

For glaze, in a small saucepan combine the jalapeño jelly, lime juice, and garlic. Cook and stir over medium heat until jelly is melted. Remove from heat.

In a small covered saucepan cook onions in a small amount of boiling water for 3 minutes. Add squash; cook for 1 minute more. Drain. Trim fat from steak. Cut steak into 1-inch cubes. On four 12-inch skewers alternately thread steak, onions, squash, tomatillos, and sweet pepper.

Grill the kabobs on the rack of an uncovered grill directly over medium heat for 12 to 14 minutes or until steak is cooked to desired doneness, turning kabobs once and brushing occasionally with glaze the last 5 minutes of grilling. If desired, stir cilantro into cooked rice and serve with kabobs. Serve with any remaining glaze.

Nutrition facts per serving: 444 cal., 11 g total fat (4 g sat. fat), 76 mg chol., 71 mg sodium, 61 g carbo., 2 g fiber, 27 g pro. Daily values: 9% vit. A, 54% vit. C, 4% calcium, 27% iron

1 **10-ounce jar jalapeño pepper jelly**

2 **tablespoons lime juice**

½ **teaspoon bottled minced garlic**

4 **small purple or white boiling onions**

4 **baby pattypan squash,**
  **halved crosswise**

1 **pound boneless beef sirloin steak,**
  **cut 1 inch thick**

4 **tomatillos, husked and cut**
  **into quarters**

½ **medium red or green sweet**
  **pepper, cut into 1-inch squares**

  **Fresh snipped cilantro (optional)**

  **Hot cooked rice (optional)**

# lemony flank steak

Though it's rare to utter the words "light" and "beef" in the same breath, this refreshingly different dish is undeniably both. Lots of fresh lemon flavors the super-lean flank steak or top sirloin. Serve it with a side of grilled or steamed asparagus.

36

1  1½-pound beef flank steak or boneless beef top sirloin steak

1  teaspoon finely shredded lemon peel

½  cup lemon juice

2  tablespoons sugar

2  tablespoons soy sauce

2  teaspoons snipped fresh oregano or ½ teaspoon dried oregano, crushed

⅛  teaspoon pepper

Lemon slices (optional)

Fresh oregano leaves (optional)

**Prep: 15 minutes   Marinate: 2 hours   Grill: 12 minutes**
**Makes 3 servings**

Trim fat from steak. Score steak on both sides by making shallow cuts at 1-inch intervals in a diamond pattern. Place steak in a plastic bag set in a shallow dish. For marinade, combine the lemon peel, lemon juice, sugar, soy sauce, oregano, and pepper. Pour over steak; close bag. Marinate in refrigerator at least 2 hours or overnight.

Drain steak, reserving marinade. Grill steak on the rack of an uncovered grill directly over medium heat to desired doneness, turning and brushing once with marinade halfway through cooking. (Allow 12 to 14 minutes for medium doneness.) Discard any remaining marinade.

To serve, thinly slice steak diagonally across the grain. If desired, garnish with lemon slices and fresh oregano leaves.

Nutrition facts per serving: 267 cal., 12 g total fat (5 g sat. fat), 80 mg chol., 357 mg sodium, 5 g carbo., 0 g fiber, 33 g pro. Daily values: 12% vit. C, 1% calcium, 21% iron

# peppercorn beef

These savory steaks get much of their great flavor from the bite of fresh-cracked pepper. Using all black peppercorns works just fine, but a mix of black (the hottest), white (gentler), and pink (faintly sweet) peppercorns offers more variety of flavors.

4 beef tenderloin steaks (about 1½ pounds total) or 1 to 1½ pounds boneless beef sirloin steak, cut 1¼ inches thick

⅓ cup bottled oil and vinegar salad dressing

⅓ cup dry red wine

¼ cup snipped fresh garlic chives or ¼ cup snipped fresh chives plus 1 teaspoon bottled minced garlic

1 teaspoon cracked multicolor or black peppercorns

**Prep: 12 minutes   Marinate: 15 minutes   Grill: 14 minutes**
**Makes 4 servings**

Trim any fat from steak(s). Place meat in a plastic bag set in a shallow dish. For marinade, combine the salad dressing, wine, garlic chives, and pepper. Pour over steaks; close bag. Marinate meat at room temperature for 15 minutes, turning bag once. (Or, marinate steaks in refrigerator for 8 to 12 hours.)

Drain the steak(s), reserving marinade. Grill meat on the rack of an uncovered grill directly over medium heat to desired doneness, turning and brushing once with marinade halfway through cooking. (Allow 14 to 18 minutes for medium-rare and 18 to 22 minutes for medium doneness.) Discard any remaining marinade. If using sirloin steak, cut steak into 4 serving-size pieces.

Nutrition facts per serving: 287 cal., 16 g total fat (5 g sat. fat), 96 mg chol., 218 mg sodium, 1 g carbo., 0 g fiber, 32 g pro. Daily values: 2% vit. C, 28% iron

# southwest steak

Marinating the meat overnight in an aromatic mélange of fresh ingredients makes this steak doubly good: It intensifies the delicious flavors, and the dish can be ready to eat in a flash on a weeknight. Serve it with cilantro-flecked rice or warmed flour tortillas.

**Prep: 20 minutes    Marinate: 6 hours    Grill: 14 minutes**
**Makes 4 servings**

Trim fat from steak. Place steak in a plastic bag set in a shallow dish. For marinade, combine onion, lime juice, 2 tablespoons of the cilantro, the jalapeño peppers, water, oil, cumin, garlic, red pepper, and salt. Pour over steak; close bag. Marinate in refrigerator for 6 hours or overnight, turning bag occasionally.

Drain steak, reserving marinade. Grill steak on the rack of an uncovered grill directly over medium heat to desired doneness, turning once and brushing occasionally with marinade up to the last 5 minutes. (Allow 14 to 18 minutes for medium-rare and 18 to 22 minutes for medium doneness.) Discard any remaining marinade. Sprinkle steak with the remaining 2 tablespoons cilantro. If desired, stir additional cilantro into cooked rice and serve with steak.

Nutrition facts per serving: 256 cal., 15 g total fat (5 g sat. fat), 76 mg chol., 148 mg sodium, 3 g carbo., 0 g fiber, 26 g pro. Daily values: 1% vit. A, 27% vit. C, 1% calcium, 22% iron

1  pound boneless beef sirloin steak, cut 1¼ to 1½ inches thick

1  medium onion, chopped

⅓  cup lime juice

¼  cup snipped fresh cilantro

3  fresh jalapeño peppers, seeded and finely chopped

3  tablespoons water

2  tablespoons cooking oil

1  teaspoon ground cumin

1  teaspoon bottled minced garlic

½  teaspoon ground red pepper

¼  teaspoon salt

Snipped fresh cilantro (optional)

Hot cooked rice (optional)

# spanish meat loaves

Humble meat loaf goes haute cuisine, but retains its almost-universal appeal. These miniature loaves, flavored with pimiento-stuffed green olives and flat-leaf parsley and glazed with sweet-hot jalapeño pepper jelly, will charm their way into your repertoire.

- **1** beaten egg
- **¾** cup quick-cooking rolled oats
- **½** cup pimiento-stuffed green olives, sliced
- **¼** cup snipped Italian flat-leaf parsley or curly parsley
- **¼** cup tomato paste
- **¼** teaspoon pepper
- **1** pound lean ground beef
- **¼** cup jalapeño pepper jelly or apple jelly, melted
- **1** medium tomato, chopped
- **⅓** cup chunky salsa
- **¼** cup chopped, seeded cucumber
- **2** tablespoons sliced pimiento-stuffed green olives (optional)
- Lettuce leaves
- **8** thin slices bread, toasted (optional)

**Prep: 15 minutes    Grill: 18 minutes**
**Makes 4 servings**

In a medium bowl combine the egg, rolled oats, the ½ cup olives, the parsley, tomato paste, and pepper. Add the ground beef; mix well. Form into four 4×2½×1-inch meat loaves.

Grill meat loaves on the rack of an uncovered grill directly over medium heat for 16 to 18 minutes or until meat is no longer pink, turning once. Brush with melted jelly; grill for 2 minutes more.

Meanwhile, for relish, in a small bowl combine the tomato, salsa, cucumber, and, if desired, the 2 tablespoons olives. Divide the lettuce and, if desired, bread slices among 4 dinner plates. Top with the meat loaves and relish.

Nutrition facts per serving: 362 cal., 16 g total fat (5 g sat. fat), 125 mg chol., 479 mg sodium, 31 g carbo., 2 g fiber, 26 g pro. Daily values: 15% vit. A, 47% vit. C, 4% calcium, 30% iron

# indian beef patties

**Try one of the many Indian breads with these meat patties. Look for chapati or roti (soft, unleavened, whole wheat bread); pappadam (paper-thin lentil crackers spiked with black peppercorns); or naan (soft, yeasted flatbread baked in a tandoor, or clay oven).**

42

½ **cup plain low-fat yogurt**

⅓ **cup chopped, seeded cucumber**

¼ **cup finely chopped onion**

1 **medium fresh jalapeño pepper, seeded and chopped, or 2 tablespoons canned diced green chili peppers**

1 **tablespoon snipped fresh mint or 1 teaspoon dried mint, crushed**

½ **teaspoon ground cumin**

½ **teaspoon bottled minced garlic or ⅛ teaspoon garlic powder**

¼ **teaspoon salt**

8 **ounces lean ground beef, pork, or turkey**

**Prep: 15 minutes    Grill: 14 minutes**
**Makes 2 servings**

For sauce, in a small bowl stir together yogurt and cucumber. Cover and refrigerate until ready to serve.

In a medium bowl combine the onion, jalapeño pepper, mint, cumin, garlic, and salt. Add the ground beef; mix well. Form mixture into two ¾-inch-thick patties. Grill patties on the rack of an uncovered grill directly over medium heat for 14 to 18 minutes or until meat is no longer pink, turning once. Serve the sauce over patties.

Nutrition facts per serving: 238 cal., 12 g total fat (5 g sat. fat), 75 mg chol., 353 mg sodium, 8 g carbo., 1 g fiber, 24 g pro. Daily values: 2% vit. A, 27% vit. C, 11% calcium, 22% iron

## direct versus **indirect**

Direct grilling means food is placed on the rack directly over the coals. This method is preferred for fast-cooking foods (burgers, steaks, boneless chicken pieces, fish, and seafood). Indirect grilling means that a covered grill acts as an oven. A disposable drip pan is placed in the center of the charcoal grate and hot coals are arranged around it. This method is used for slower-cooking foods (roasts, whole or bone-in poultry, or ribs; or foods that may burn over direct heat, for example, rubs with fresh herbs or high-sugar sauces). Because of their speed, most of the recipes in this book call for direct grilling. See grilling charts on pages 90 to 93 for timings.

# beef & swiss sandwiches

These sandwiches are a tantalizing fusion of juicy, horseradish-mustard-marinated steak on toasted rolls; tangy, melting Swiss cheese; and crunchy cabbage slaw flavored with caramelized sweet onions. Delicious!

43

**Prep: 15 minutes    Marinate: 6 hours    Grill: 12 minutes**
**Makes 6 servings**

Trim fat from steak. Score the steak by making shallow cuts at 1-inch intervals in a diamond pattern. Place steak and onion in a plastic bag set in a shallow dish. Combine dressing and mustard. Add to bag; close bag. Marinate in refrigerator for 6 to 24 hours, turning bag occasionally.

Drain steak and onion, reserving marinade. Fold a 24×18-inch piece of heavy foil in half to make a 12×18-inch rectangle. Place onion in the center of foil. Drizzle 2 tablespoons of the marinade over onion. Bring up 2 opposite edges of foil; seal with a double fold. Fold remaining ends to completely enclose onion, leaving space for steam to build.

Grill steak and onion on the rack of an uncovered grill directly over medium heat until steak is cooked to desired doneness, turning steak and onion and brushing steak once with marinade halfway through cooking. (Allow 12 to 14 minutes for medium doneness.) Discard any remaining marinade. Toast the rolls on the grill.

To serve, thinly slice steak diagonally across grain. Toss together onion and cabbage. Fill rolls with steak and onion mixture. Top with cheese.

Nutrition facts per serving: 394 cal., 22 g total fat (7 g sat. fat), 53 mg chol., 530 mg sodium, 25 g carbo., 1 g fiber, 24 g pro. Daily values: 18% vit. A, 16% vit. C, 19% calcium, 17% iron

- 1  1- to 1¼-pound beef flank steak
- 1  medium sweet onion (such as Vidalia or Walla Walla), thinly sliced
- ½  cup bottled clear Italian salad dressing or oil and vinegar salad dressing
- 2  tablespoons horseradish mustard
- 6  French-style rolls, split
- 1½  cups packaged shredded cabbage with carrot (coleslaw mix) or shredded red cabbage
- 4  ounces thinly sliced Swiss cheese

# perfect
# pork & lamb

# southwest pork chops with corn salsa

In late summer, when the corn is at its sweetest and the tomatoes are at their juiciest, these meaty pork chops crowned with a colorful, chunky salsa are unsurpassed for the freshest tastes of the season's best.

**Prep: 20 minutes    Grill: 8 minutes**
**Makes 4 servings**

For sauce, combine 3 tablespoons of the vinegar, 1 tablespoon of the cilantro, and the olive oil. For salsa, thaw corn, if frozen. In a medium bowl combine corn, tomatoes, green onions, jalapeño pepper, the remaining vinegar, and the remaining cilantro. Set aside.

Trim fat from chops. Grill chops on rack of an uncovered grill directly over medium heat for 8 to 11 minutes or until chops are slightly pink in center and juices run clear, turning once and brushing occasionally with sauce. If desired, serve chops on cactus leaves. Serve with salsa.

Nutrition facts per serving: 201 cal., 9 g total fat (3 g sat. fat), 51 mg chol., 51 mg sodium, 14 g carbo., 2 g fiber, 18 g pro. Daily values: 7% vit. A, 35% vit. C, 8% iron

¼  cup white wine vinegar

3  tablespoons snipped fresh cilantro

1  teaspoon olive oil

1  cup fresh or frozen whole
    kernel corn

3  plum-shaped tomatoes, chopped

½  cup thinly sliced green onions

1  small fresh jalapeño pepper,
    seeded and minced

4  center-cut pork loin chops, cut
    ¾ inch thick

    Cactus leaves (optional)

## particular about pork

Today's pork is leaner—and therefore lower in fat and calories—than ever before. Because there is so little fat, pork requires a little extra attention when being grilled to ensure tender, juicy meat. Closely check timings and temperatures in the recipes. Cook roasts and chops from the loin and rib sections to an internal temperature of 160° (medium-well) or 170° (well done). Cook ground pork and less-tender cuts such as sirloin or loin blade roasts and chops to 170° (well done) or until no pink remains.

# currant-glazed
## pork burgers

Currant jelly and cloves—favorites for flavoring the Christmas ham—go casual for everyday eating in these savory pork burgers. Choose leafy greens such as Bibb, red-tip leaf, or romaine lettuce as a crisp accompaniment.

46

¼  **cup currant jelly**

3  **tablespoons catsup**

1  **tablespoon vinegar**

⅛  **teaspoon ground cinnamon**

   **Dash ground cloves**

1  **beaten egg**

3  **tablespoons fine dry bread crumbs**

2  **tablespoons chopped onion**

2  **tablespoons milk**

¼  **teaspoon salt**

¼  **teaspoon dried thyme, crushed**

⅛  **teaspoon pepper**

1  **pound lean ground pork**

4  **whole wheat hamburger buns, split**

4  **lettuce leaves**

**Prep: 15 minutes   Grill: 14 minutes**
**Makes 4 servings**

For sauce, in a small saucepan combine currant jelly, catsup, vinegar, cinnamon, and cloves. Cook and stir just until boiling. Remove from heat and keep warm.

In a medium bowl combine egg, bread crumbs, onion, milk, salt, thyme, and pepper. Add the ground pork; mix well. Form mixture into four ¾-inch-thick patties.

Grill patties on the rack of an uncovered grill directly over medium heat for 14 to 18 minutes or until meat is no longer pink, turning once. Toast the hamburger buns on the grill.

Place lettuce on bottoms of buns; top with patties. Spoon the sauce evenly over patties.

Nutrition facts per serving: 347 cal., 11 g total fat (4 g sat. fat), 107 mg chol., 612 mg sodium, 43 g carbo., 3 g fiber, 21 g pro. Daily values: 5% vit. A, 6% vit. C, 6% calcium, 18% iron

# smoky pork &
# mushroom kabobs

These kabobs boast the flavors of fall: maple syrup, cider vinegar, hickory smoke, and sweet-tart apples. Choose a good cooking apple, such as Rome Beauty, York Imperial, Newtown Pippin, or Granny Smith.

**Prep: 15 minutes    Marinate: 10 minutes    Grill: 14 minutes**
**Makes 4 servings**

Trim fat from pork. Cut pork into 1½-inch cubes. Place the pork, mushrooms, apples, and onion in a plastic bag set in a shallow dish. For marinade, combine the syrup, tomato paste, vinegar, smoke flavoring, and pepper. Reserve ¼ cup marinade for dipping sauce. Pour remaining marinade over the pork, mushrooms, apples, onion; close bag. Marinate in refrigerator at least 10 minutes or up to 4 hours, turning the bag once.

Drain the pork mixture, reserving marinade. On four 12-inch skewers alternately thread pork, mushrooms, apples, and onion.

Grill kabobs on the greased rack of an uncovered grill directly over medium heat for 14 to 16 minutes or until the pork is slightly pink in the center and juices run clear, turning and brushing once with reserved marinade halfway through grilling. Serve with dipping sauce.

Nutrition facts per serving: 261 cal., 8 g total fat (3 g sat. fat), 51 mg chol., 54 mg sodium,
32 g carbo., 3 g fiber, 18 g pro. Daily values: 4% vit. A, 23% vit. C, 1% calcium, 16% iron

1  pound lean boneless pork

8  ounces fresh mushroom caps

2  medium apples, cored and
    quartered

1  medium onion, cut into wedges

¼  cup maple-flavored syrup

¼  cup tomato paste

2  tablespoons cider vinegar

¼  to ½ teaspoon hickory smoke
    flavoring

⅛  teaspoon pepper

# canadian bacon pizza

Pizza—on the grill? You bet! The intense, direct heat of the grill approximates that of a wood-fired pizza oven, imparting the pie's veggies and cheese with a pleasing smoke flavor, the Canadian bacon with real sizzle, and the crust with a delightful crunch.

**Prep: 20 minutes  Grill: 8 minutes**
**Makes 4 servings**

Drain artichoke hearts, reserving marinade. Halve artichoke hearts lengthwise; set aside.

Brush the bread shells with some of the reserved marinade. Sprinkle fontina cheese over shells. Divide artichoke hearts, Canadian-style bacon, tomatoes, feta cheese, green onion, and oregano among shells.

Transfer the bread shells to a large piece of double-thickness foil. In a grill with a cover place foil with bread shells on the rack directly over medium heat. Cover and grill about 8 minutes or until cheese is melted and pizza is heated through.

Nutrition facts per serving: 465 cal., 19 g total fat (6 g sat. fat), 44 mg chol., 1,264 mg sodium, 56 g carbo., 2 g fiber, 23 g pro. Daily values: 13% vit. A, 34% vit. C, 24% calcium, 19% iron

1  6-ounce jar marinated
    artichoke hearts

4  6-inch Italian bread shells (Boboli)

½  cup shredded fontina or
    mozzarella cheese (2 ounces)

4  slices Canadian-style bacon,
    cut into strips (2 ounces)

2  plum-shaped tomatoes, sliced

¼  cup crumbled feta cheese
    (1 ounce)

1  green onion, thinly sliced

2  teaspoons snipped fresh oregano
    or basil

# teriyaki pork salad

In Japanese *teri* means glazed and *yaki* means baked or broiled. The sugar in the marinade caramelizes as it is grilled, giving the pork a beautiful shine. Serve it over mixed greens with peppery radishes, a tasty contrast to the sweetness of the sauce.

4 boneless pork top loin chops, cut ¾ inch thick

⅓ cup rice vinegar

⅓ cup orange juice

2 tablespoons reduced-sodium teriyaki sauce

1 tablespoon peanut oil or salad oil

1 teaspoon sesame seed, toasted

1 teaspoon bottled minced garlic

6 cups packaged torn mixed salad greens

¾ cup sliced red radishes

¼ cup thinly sliced green onions

**Prep: 15 minutes   Marinate: 20 minutes   Grill: 8 minutes**
**Makes 4 servings**

Trim fat from chops. Place chops in a plastic bag set in a shallow dish. For marinade, whisk together vinegar, orange juice, teriyaki sauce, oil, sesame seed, and garlic. Reserve half for dressing. Pour the remaining marinade over the chops; close bag. Marinate in refrigerator at least 20 minutes or up to 8 hours, turning bag occasionally.

Drain chops, reserving marinade. Grill the chops on the rack of an uncovered grill directly over medium heat for 8 to 11 minutes or until chops are slightly pink in center and the juices run clear, turning and brushing once with marinade halfway through grilling. Discard any remaining marinade.

Divide greens, radishes, and green onions among 4 dinner plates. Thinly slice pork diagonally and arrange on top of greens. Drizzle with dressing.

Nutrition facts per serving: 199 cal., 11 g total fat (3 g sat. fat), 51 mg chol., 172 mg sodium, 7 g carbo., 1 g fiber, 18 g pro. Daily values: 4% vit. A, 28% vit. C, 2% calcium, 8% iron

# peach-mustard
## glazed ham

**Head south to a sunnier clime at dinnertime. Fresh peaches and ham—two Southern specialties—make perfect partners in this sweet and smoky dish. Serve it with warm cornbread spread with butter and honey.**

**Prep: 5 minutes    Grill: 12 minutes**
**Makes 4 servings**

For glaze, in a bowl combine brown sugar and mustard. Gradually whisk in nectar until smooth. To prevent ham from curling, make shallow cuts around the edge at 1-inch intervals. Brush one side of ham with glaze. Grill ham, glazed-side down, on the greased rack of an uncovered grill directly over medium-hot heat for 6 minutes. Turn ham. Add peaches and peppers. Brush ham, peaches, and peppers with glaze. Grill for 6 to 10 minutes or until heated through, brushing occasionally with glaze.

Nutrition facts per serving: 284 cal., 7 g total fat (2 g sat. fat), 60 mg chol., 1,468 mg sodium, 31 g carbo., 3 g fiber, 26 g pro. Daily values: 11% vit. A, 94% vit. C, 2% calcium, 15% iron

- 2 **tablespoons brown sugar**
- 2 **tablespoons spicy brown mustard**
- ⅓ **cup peach or apricot nectar**
- 1 **1-pound cooked ham slice, cut ¾ to 1 inch thick**
- 4 **medium peaches, peeled and halved lengthwise**
- 2 **small green and/or red sweet peppers, each cut crosswise into 4 rings**

### fired up about smoking (on the grill)

You don't need a smoker to smoke meats. Adding wood chips or chunks to your briquettes gives grilled foods a special wood-smoked aroma and flavor. Good wood-chip choices include mesquite, alder, hickory, oak, and fruitwoods such as apple, cherry, and peach. Read the package labels; it's likely you'll need to soak the chips before you use them so they'll smoke—not burn. If you have a gas grill, try charcoal-flavored briquettes made specifically for gas grills. The hardwoods they contain—such as mesquite and hickory—impart a wood-smoked taste and aroma to grilled foods.

# jamaican pork chops with melon salsa

The jerk cooks of Jamaica may use dry rubs or wet marinades but the central ingredient in all jerk seasoning is allspice (along with fiery Scotch bonnet chilies and thyme), which grows in abundance on the sunny island.

- 1 cup chopped honeydew melon
- 1 cup chopped cantaloupe
- 1 tablespoon snipped fresh mint
- 1 tablespoon honey
- 4 boneless pork top loin chops, cut ¾ to 1 inch thick
- 4 teaspoons Jamaican jerk seasoning
   Fresh mint and/or star anise (optional)

**Prep: 15 minutes   Grill: 8 minutes**
**Makes 4 servings**

For salsa, in a bowl combine honeydew, cantaloupe, the 1 tablespoon mint, and the honey. Cover and refrigerate until ready to serve.

Trim fat from chops. Rub both sides of the chops with Jamaican jerk seasoning. Grill chops on the rack of an uncovered grill directly over medium heat for 8 to 12 minutes or until the chops are slightly pink in center and juices run clear. Serve salsa with chops. If desired, garnish with star anise or additional mint.

Nutrition facts per serving: 189 cal., 8 g total fat (3 g sat. fat), 51 mg chol., 231 mg sodium, 13 g carbo., 1 g fiber, 17 g pro. Daily values: 22% vit. A, 48% vit. C, 2% calcium, 10% iron

# lamb burgers with feta & mint

Hold the catsup and mustard! You won't need either on these decidedly different burgers. The tang of feta cheese and the refreshing flavor of fresh mint enliven these peppered lamb (or beef) burgers.

54

1  pound lean ground lamb or beef

2  teaspoons freshly ground pepper

4  lettuce leaves

4  kaiser rolls, split

½  cup crumbled feta cheese
    (2 ounces)

4  tomato slices

1  tablespoon snipped fresh mint

**Prep: 15 minutes    Grill: 14 minutes**
**Makes 4 servings**

Form ground lamb into four ¾-inch-thick patties. Press pepper evenly into patties. Grill patties on the greased rack of an uncovered grill directly over medium heat for 14 to 18 minutes or until meat is no longer pink, turning once.

Place lettuce on bottoms of rolls. Top with patties, feta cheese, tomato slices, and mint.

Nutrition facts per serving: 435 cal., 21 g total fat (9 g sat. fat), 88 mg chol., 535 mg sodium, 33 g carbo., 1 g fiber, 28 g pro. Daily values: 4% vit. A, 11% vit. C, 12% calcium, 27% iron

## is it **done** yet?

Because of the high temperature of the grill, meats can cook quickly on the outside—in fact, they can burn—before the inside is done. You can determine doneness of steaks by making a small slit near the bone and checking for color. For boneless steaks, make a slit near the center. Ground-meat patties with no other added ingredients should be cooked at least until the centers are brownish pink (medium doneness). Ground-meat patties with added ingredients—eggs, bread crumbs, onions, or liquid— should be cooked to 170° or until no pink remains. Cut into the patty to see that the color of the center of the patty is brown.

# greek-inspired
## lamb pockets

Be a dinnertime hero with a meal-in-a-pocket that will win you applause. Meaty lamb leg or shoulder is marinated in balsamic vinegar, pepper, and fresh herbs, quick-grilled to keep it juicy, then tucked into a pita and topped with a creamy yogurt sauce.

**55**

**Prep: 20 minutes   Marinate: 10 minutes   Grill: 10 minutes
Makes 4 servings**

Trim fat from lamb. Cut lamb into 2×1-inch thin strips. Place lamb in a plastic bag set in a shallow dish. For marinade, combine the vinegar, savory, and pepper. Pour marinade over lamb; close bag. Marinate in the refrigerator at least 10 minutes or up to 4 hours, turning bag once. Meanwhile, for sauce, in a medium bowl combine yogurt, cucumber, tomatoes, and onion. Cover and refrigerate until ready to serve. Wrap pita rounds in foil. Set aside.

Drain lamb, reserving marinade. On four 12-inch skewers thread lamb, accordion-style. Grill kabobs on the rack of an uncovered grill directly over medium heat for 10 to 12 minutes or to desired doneness, turning kabobs once and brushing occasionally with marinade up to the last 5 minutes. Place the pita rounds on grill rack next to the kabobs the last 5 minutes of grilling. Discard any remaining marinade.

Cut pita rounds in half crosswise. Spoon the sauce into pita halves and fill with lamb strips.

Nutrition facts per serving: 361 cal., 8 g total fat (3 g sat. fat), 61 mg chol., 430 mg sodium, 46 g carbo., 1 g fiber, 28 g pro. Daily values: 3% vit. A, 20% vit. C, 10% calcium, 15% iron

1  pound boneless lamb leg or shoulder

¼  cup balsamic vinegar

1  tablespoon snipped fresh savory or 1 teaspoon dried savory, crushed

½  teaspoon pepper

1  8-ounce carton plain low-fat or fat-free yogurt

1  small cucumber, peeled, seeded, and chopped (¾ cup)

2  plum-shaped tomatoes, chopped

1  small onion, finely chopped

4  whole wheat pita bread rounds

# apple-glazed lamb chops

Lamb chops make an elegant quick-to-fix dish, and these cinnamon- and apple-spiced lamb chops are the ultimate company fare. Add a side of couscous tossed with fresh mint and finish with a scoop of sorbet for a weekday dinner with friends.

**Prep: 15 minutes   Grill: 14 minutes**
**Makes 4 servings**

For glaze, in a small saucepan heat and stir apple jelly, green onion, soy sauce, lemon juice, curry powder, cinnamon, and red pepper over medium heat until bubbly. Remove from heat. Remove seeds from apple slices. Brush apples with lemon juice. Set aside.

Trim fat from chops. Grill chops on the rack of an uncovered grill directly over medium heat until chops are cooked to desired doneness, turning and brushing once with glaze. (Allow 10 to 14 minutes for medium-rare and 14 to 16 minutes for medium doneness.) Place apples on grill rack next to chops the last 5 minutes of grilling, turning and brushing once with glaze.

If desired, serve chops and apples with couscous. Sprinkle with mint.

Nutrition facts per serving: 385 cal., 14 g total fat (5 g sat. fat), 133 mg chol., 378 mg sodium, 20 g carbo., 1 g fiber, 43 g pro. Daily values: 1% vit. A, 11% vit. C, 3% calcium, 23% iron

3 tablespoons apple jelly

1 green onion, thinly sliced

1 tablespoon soy sauce

2 teaspoons lemon juice

⅛ teaspoon curry powder

Dash ground cinnamon

Dash ground red pepper

2 small red and/or green apples, cut crosswise into ¼-inch-thick slices

Lemon juice

8 lamb loin chops, cut 1 inch thick

Hot cooked couscous (optional)

1 tablespoon snipped fresh mint

so easy
seafood

# salmon with fresh pineapple salsa

You don't need to have a party—just a weeknight dinner will do—to enjoy the sweet-hot fruit salsa that's as pretty as a sprinkling of confetti on top of this grilled salmon fillet. Serve it with hot cooked rice.

**Start to finish: 30 minutes**
**Makes 4 servings**

For salsa, in a medium bowl combine pineapple, sweet pepper, onion, 2 tablespoons of the lime juice, the jalapeño pepper, cilantro, and honey. Set aside.

Rinse fish; pat dry. Brush both sides of fish with the remaining lime juice and sprinkle with cumin. Place fish in a well-greased wire grill basket. Grill fish on the rack of an uncovered grill directly over medium heat for 8 to 12 minutes or until fish flakes easily with a fork, turning basket once. Cut fish into 4 serving-size pieces. Serve with the salsa.

Nutrition facts per serving: 170 cal., 4 g total fat (1 g sat. fat), 20 mg chol., 70 mg sodium, 17 g carbo., 1 g fiber, 17 g pro. Daily values: 16% vit. A, 75% vit. C, 1% calcium, 9% iron

2 cups coarsely chopped fresh pineapple

½ cup chopped red sweet pepper

¼ cup finely chopped red onion

3 tablespoons lime juice

1 small fresh jalapeño pepper, seeded and finely chopped

1 tablespoon snipped fresh cilantro or chives

1 tablespoon honey

1 1-pound fresh skinless salmon fillet, 1 inch thick

¼ teaspoon ground cumin

# salmon with cucumber kabobs

Cooked cucumbers provide a pleasant change of pace on these kabobs. Though their characteristic crispness disappears with cooking, their delicacy does not, making them a perfect companion for light and elegant fish dishes.

4 6- to 8-ounce fresh skinless
  salmon fillets, ½ to 1 inch thick

⅓ cup lemon juice

1 tablespoon olive oil or cooking oil

2 teaspoons snipped fresh tarragon

1 medium cucumber, halved
  lengthwise and sliced 1 inch thick

1 medium red onion, cut into wedges

8 cherry tomatoes

  Hot cooked rice (optional)

Prep: 15 minutes   Marinate: 10 minutes   Grill: 8 minutes
Makes 4 servings

Rinse fish; pat dry. Place fish in a plastic bag set in a shallow dish. For marinade, combine lemon juice, oil, and tarragon. Reserve half for basting. Pour remaining marinade over fish; close bag. Marinate at room temperature for 10 to 20 minutes. Meanwhile, on four 10-inch skewers alternately thread cucumber and onion.

Drain fish, discarding marinade. Place fish in a well-greased wire grill basket. Grill the fish and vegetables on the rack of an uncovered grill directly over medium heat until fish flakes easily with a fork and vegetables are tender, turning basket and vegetables once and brushing occasionally with basting sauce. (Allow 4 to 6 minutes per ½-inch thickness of fish and 8 to 12 minutes for vegetables.) Add tomatoes to ends of kabobs the last 2 minutes of grilling.

If desired, serve fish and vegetables with rice.

Nutrition facts per serving: 201 cal., 8 g total fat (2 g sat. fat), 31 mg chol., 106 mg sodium, 6 g carbo., 1 g fiber, 25 g pro. Daily values: 6% vit. A, 25% vit. C, 2% calcium, 9% iron

# panzanella with grilled tuna

Pané means bread in Italian, and making panzanella is a wonderful way to use bread that's not as fresh as just-baked but still too good to throw away. Bread salad may be an economical way to use up leftover bread, but it's simply delicious, too.

**Prep: 20 minutes    Grill: 4 minutes    Stand: 5 minutes
Makes 4 servings**

For sauce, in a small bowl combine vinaigrette and rosemary. Reserve 2 tablespoons for dressing.

Rinse fish; pat dry. Grill fish on the greased rack of an uncovered grill directly over medium heat until fish flakes easily with a fork, turning and brushing once with remaining sauce. (Allow 4 to 6 minutes per ½-inch thickness of fish.)

Meanwhile, in a large salad bowl combine greens, broccoli, tomatoes, and green onions. Flake fish; add to greens mixture. Drizzle with the dressing; toss gently to coat. Add bread cubes; toss gently to combine. Let stand for 5 minutes before serving. If desired, sprinkle with cheese.

Nutrition facts per serving: 380 cal., 17 g total fat (3 g sat. fat), 47 mg chol., 608 mg sodium, 24 g carbo., 2 g fiber, 33 g pro. Daily values: 82% vit. A, 69% vit. C, 5% calcium, 19% iron

- ½ **cup bottled balsamic vinaigrette or red wine vinegar salad dressing**
- ½ **teaspoon finely snipped fresh rosemary**
- 1 **pound fresh tuna steaks, ½ to 1 inch thick**
- 2 **cups packaged torn mixed salad greens**
- 1½ **cups broccoli flowerets**
- 2 **small tomatoes, chopped**
- ¼ **cup thinly sliced green onions**
- 4 **cups 1-inch cubes day-old Italian bread**

  **Finely shredded Parmesan cheese (optional)**

# shark with nectarine salsa

Shark usually is sold as fillets, but if you can't find it, orange roughy makes a fine substitute. Orange roughy, found in the waters near New Zealand and Australia, has firm white flesh with a mild flavor. However, any mild white fish is acceptable.

**63**

**Prep: 30 minutes   Grill: 8 minutes**
**Makes 4 servings**

For salsa, in a bowl combine nectarine, cucumber, kiwifruit, onions, orange juice, and vinegar. Cover and refrigerate until ready to serve.

Rinse fish; pat dry. Rub oil over both sides of fish and sprinkle with pepper. Place fish in a well-greased wire grill basket. Grill fish on the rack of an uncovered grill directly over medium heat for 8 to 12 minutes or until fish flakes easily with a fork, turning basket once. Spoon the salsa over fish. Cut fish into 4 serving-size pieces.

Nutrition facts per serving: 158 cal., 3 g total fat (1 g sat. fat), 60 mg chol., 94 mg sodium, 10 g carbo., 1 g fiber, 22 g pro. Daily values: 6% vit. A, 55% vit. C, 3% calcium, 5% iron

- 1 **ripe nectarine, cut into ½-inch pieces**
- 1 **small cucumber, seeded and cut into ½-inch pieces**
- 1 **ripe kiwifruit, peeled and cut into ½-inch pieces**
- ¼ **cup thinly sliced green onions**
- 3 **tablespoons orange juice**
- 1 **tablespoon white wine vinegar**
- 1 **1-pound fresh shark or orange roughy fillet, 1 inch thick**
- 1 **teaspoon olive oil**
- ½ **teaspoon freshly ground pepper**

## tips for grilling fish

Much of the appeal of fish is that it is so tender and delicate. Fish is a great candidate for the grill—with a little extra care to prevent it from breaking apart. It helps to place fish on foil (and use a wide spatula if you must turn it) or in a grill basket when grilling. Grill baskets are intended for direct grilling only—most grill-basket handles can't take the heat of indirect cooking on a covered grill. Be sure to lightly grease or brush the foil or basket with cooking oil before adding the fish. Firmer-textured fish steaks can be grilled on a greased grill rack.

# grouper with red pepper sauce

When you're in the mood for fish, look to this member of the sea bass family with its mild, sweet flavor. Gild the lily with this exceptional red pepper-tomato sauce.

1 large red sweet pepper, chopped

1 tablespoon margarine or butter

2 medium tomatoes, peeled, seeded, and chopped

1 tablespoon sugar

1 teaspoon red wine vinegar

¼ teaspoon salt

⅛ teaspoon garlic powder

Dash ground red pepper

2 tablespoons lemon juice

1 tablespoon olive oil

¼ teaspoon dried rosemary, crushed

4 4-ounce fresh grouper fillets, ½ to 1 inch thick

**Prep: 25 minutes    Grill: 4 minutes**
**Makes 4 servings**

For sauce, in a medium saucepan cook sweet pepper in hot margarine or butter over medium heat until tender. Stir in tomatoes, sugar, vinegar, salt, garlic powder, and ground red pepper. Cook for 5 minutes, stirring occasionally. Transfer mixture to a blender container or food processor bowl. Cover and blend or process until smooth. Return to saucepan; cover and keep warm.*

In a small bowl combine the lemon juice, oil, and rosemary. Rinse fish; pat dry. Brush both sides of fish with lemon mixture. Place fish in a well-greased wire grill basket. Grill fish on the rack of an uncovered grill directly over medium heat until fish flakes easily with a fork, turning basket once. (Allow 4 to 6 minutes per ½-inch thickness of fish.) Serve sauce with fish.

Nutrition facts per serving: 194 cal., 8 g total fat (1 g sat. fat), 60 mg chol., 266 mg sodium, 9 g carbo., 1 g fiber, 22 g pro. Daily values: 27% vit. A, 97% vit. C, 2% calcium, 5% iron

*Note: If desired, you may prepare the sauce ahead of time and refrigerate until ready to grill. Before serving, reheat the sauce in a saucepan.*

# blackened catfish
# with roasted potatoes

**Catch a pan-fried Cajun classic and cook it on your grill! This version of a Southern favorite is served alongside tiny new potatoes, carrots, and onions roasted in olive oil and zippy hot pepper sauce.**

**Prep: 20 minutes   Grill: 35 minutes**
**Makes 4 servings**

Fold a 48×18-inch piece of heavy foil in half to make a 24×18-inch rectangle. In a large bowl combine the oil, salt, and pepper sauce. Add the potatoes, carrots, sweet pepper, and onion; toss to coat. Place in the center of foil. Bring up 2 opposite edges of foil; seal with a double fold. Fold remaining ends to completely enclose vegetables, leaving space for steam to build.

Grill vegetables on the rack of an uncovered grill directly over medium heat for 35 to 40 minutes or until potatoes and carrots are tender.

Meanwhile, thaw fish, if frozen. Rinse fish; pat dry. Sprinkle both sides of fish with Cajun seasoning and lightly spray with nonstick coating. Place fish in a well-greased wire grill basket. While the vegetables cook, place the fish on the grill rack next to the vegetables and grill until fish flakes easily with a fork, turning the basket once. (Allow 4 to 6 minutes per ½-inch thickness of fish.) To serve, sprinkle fish and vegetables with snipped chervil.

Nutrition facts per serving: 352 cal., 6 g total fat (1 g sat. fat), 42 mg chol., 266 mg sodium, 48 g carbo., 5 g fiber, 28 g pro. Daily values: 173% vit. A, 63% vit. C, 7% calcium, 24% iron

1 tablespoon olive oil
¼ teaspoon salt
  Several dashes bottled hot pepper sauce
1½ pounds tiny new potatoes, thinly sliced
4 medium carrots, thinly sliced
1 medium green sweet pepper, cut into thin strips
1 medium onion, sliced
4 4- to 5-ounce fresh or frozen catfish or red snapper fillets, ½ to 1 inch thick
½ teaspoon Cajun seasoning
  Nonstick spray coating
1 tablespoon snipped fresh chervil or parsley

# thai-spiced scallops

In addition to the salty, sweet, sour, and spicy flavors that spark Thai cooking, this dish features one more: basil, with its peppery, clovelike flavor—and lots of it. These delicious scallops let you sample the whole spectrum of Thai tastes.

1 pound fresh or frozen sea scallops

2 medium yellow summer squash and/or zucchini, quartered lengthwise and sliced ½ inch thick

1½ cups packaged peeled baby carrots

⅔ cup bottled sweet and sour sauce

2 tablespoons snipped fresh basil

1 teaspoon Thai seasoning or five-spice powder

½ teaspoon bottled minced garlic

Start to finish: 30 minutes
Makes 4 servings

Thaw scallops, if frozen. Fold a 36×18-inch piece of heavy foil in half to make an 18×18-inch square. Place squash and carrots in center of foil. Sprinkle lightly with salt and pepper. Bring up 2 opposite edges of foil; seal with a double fold. Fold remaining ends to completely enclose the vegetables, leaving space for steam to build. Grill vegetables on the rack of an uncovered grill directly over medium heat for 15 to 20 minutes or until vegetables are crisp-tender, turning vegetables occasionally.

Meanwhile, for the sauce, in a small bowl combine the sweet and sour sauce, basil, Thai seasoning, and garlic. Transfer ¼ cup of the sauce to another bowl for basting. Reserve remaining sauce until ready to serve.

Rinse scallops; pat dry. Halve any large scallops. On four 8- to 10-inch skewers thread scallops. Place kabobs on grill rack next to vegetables the last 5 to 8 minutes of grilling or until scallops are opaque, turning and brushing once with basting sauce. Serve scallops and vegetables with the remaining sauce.

Nutrition facts per serving: 168 cal., 1 g total fat (0 g sat. fat), 34 mg chol., 370 mg sodium, 25 g carbo., 3 g fiber, 16 g pro. Daily values: 122% vit. A, 17% vit. C, 9% calcium, 18% iron

# pepper shrimp in peanut sauce

Who could resist this dish? Sweet and spicy peanut sauce dresses up whimsical bow-tie pasta, colorful and crisp sweet peppers, and best of all, the special treat of grilled shrimp.

- 1 **pound fresh or frozen medium shrimp in shells**
- 8 **ounces dried bow-tie pasta or linguine**
- ½ **cup water**
- ¼ **cup orange marmalade**
- 2 **tablespoons peanut butter**
- 2 **tablespoons soy sauce**
- 2 **teaspoons cornstarch**
- ¼ **teaspoon crushed red pepper**
- 2 **medium red, yellow, and/or green sweet peppers, cut into 1-inch pieces**

  **Chopped peanuts (optional)**

**Start to finish: 35 minutes**
**Makes 4 servings**

Thaw shrimp, if frozen. Peel and devein shrimp, leaving tails intact. Rinse shrimp; pat dry. Set aside. Cook the pasta according to package directions. Drain. Return pasta to pan; keep warm.

Meanwhile, for sauce, in a small saucepan stir together the water, orange marmalade, peanut butter, soy sauce, cornstarch, and crushed red pepper. Bring to boiling; reduce heat. Cook and stir for 2 minutes. Remove from heat and keep warm.

On eight 12-inch skewers alternately thread shrimp and sweet peppers. Grill kabobs on the rack of an uncovered grill directly over medium heat for 6 to 8 minutes or until shrimp turn pink, turning once.

To serve, add shrimp and peppers to the cooked pasta. Add the sauce; toss gently to coat. If desired, sprinkle individual servings with peanuts.

Nutrition facts per serving: 382 cal., 7 g total fat (1 g sat. fat), 180 mg chol., 718 mg sodium, 57 g carbo., 3 g fiber, 24 g pro. Daily values: 34% vit. A, 108% vit. C, 4% calcium, 33% iron

# asparagus &
# shrimp with dill butter

This lovely dish is the essence of spring (leeks, asparagus, fresh dill) and the essence of elegance (a touch of white wine and butter) in one. It's simple enough for weeknight dining but special enough to serve guests.

**69**

**Prep: 20 minutes   Grill: 15 minutes**
**Makes 4 servings**

Thaw shrimp, if frozen. Peel and devein shrimp, removing tails, if desired. Rinse shrimp; pat dry. Snap off and discard woody bases from asparagus. Bias-slice the asparagus into 2-inch pieces. In a bowl stir together the butter or margarine, dill, wine, lemon peel, salt, and pepper. Set aside.

Fold a 36×18-inch piece of heavy foil in half to make an 18×18-inch square. Place shrimp, asparagus, and leek in center of foil. Top with dill mixture. Bring up 2 opposite edges of foil; seal with a double fold. Fold remaining ends to completely enclose shrimp mixture, leaving space for steam to build.

Grill foil packet on the rack of an uncovered grill directly over medium heat about 15 minutes or until shrimp turn pink, turning packet once.

Serve the shrimp and vegetables over rice. Drizzle with the juices from foil packet.

Nutrition facts per serving: 350 cal., 13 g total fat (2 g sat. fat), 131 mg chol., 357 mg sodium, 39 g carbo., 2 g fiber, 19 g pro. Daily values: 25% vit. A, 35% vit. C, 5% calcium, 28% iron

1 pound fresh or frozen medium shrimp in shells

1 pound asparagus spears

¼ cup butter or margarine, softened

1 tablespoon snipped fresh dill or 1 teaspoon dried dillweed

1 tablespoon dry white wine

½ teaspoon finely shredded lemon peel

⅛ teaspoon salt

⅛ teaspoon pepper

1 medium leek, thinly sliced

3 cups hot cooked rice or pasta

# shrimp & tropical fruit

**Fruit cocktail goes uptown! With the addition of sweet and savory barbecued shrimp, a fresh-fruit salad of pineapple, papaya, and kiwi becomes a whole meal that hints at the warmth, sun, and fun of a tropical isle.**

**Prep: 25 minutes    Grill: 10 minutes**
**Makes 6 servings**

Thaw shrimp, if frozen. Peel and devein shrimp, leaving tails intact. Rinse shrimp; pat dry. On six 10- to 12-inch skewers thread shrimp. For sauce, in a medium bowl stir together barbecue sauce, pineapple juice, oil, and gingerroot. Brush shrimp with sauce.

Grill shrimp on the greased rack of an uncovered grill directly over medium heat for 10 to 12 minutes or until shrimp turn pink, turning once and brushing occasionally with sauce. Place pineapple on grill rack next to shrimp the last 5 minutes of grilling, turning once.

Serve shrimp and pineapple with papaya and kiwifruit. In a small saucepan heat remaining sauce to boiling; cool slightly. Pass for dipping.

Nutrition facts per serving: 199 cal., 6 g total fat (1 g sat. fat), 116 mg chol., 474 mg sodium, 21 g carbo., 1 g fiber, 14 g pro. Daily values: 13% vit. A, 115% vit. C, 5% calcium, 17% iron

1¼ pounds fresh or frozen jumbo shrimp in shells

1 cup bottled barbecue sauce

⅔ cup unsweetened pineapple juice

2 tablespoons cooking oil

4 teaspoons grated gingerroot or 1½ teaspoons ground ginger

¼ of a fresh pineapple, sliced crosswise

1 medium papaya, peeled, seeded, and cut up

3 medium kiwifruit, peeled and cut up

vibrant
vegetables

# vegetable kabobs

These crisp-tender vegetable kabobs are the essence of simplicity—a swath of rosemary-scented oil-and-vinegar dressing is their only embellishment. Threaded onto rosemary stalks, the colorful components look like jewels on a string.

**Prep: 20 minutes    Grill: 10 minutes**
**Makes 4 servings**

In a 2-quart microwave-safe casserole combine potatoes and water. Micro-cook, covered, on 100% power (high) for 5 minutes. Gently stir in sunburst squash, sweet peppers, and onions. Cook, covered, on high for 4 to 6 minutes or until nearly tender. Drain. Cool slightly.

On eight 10-inch skewers* alternately thread the sunburst squash, sweet peppers, onions, and zucchini. In a small bowl combine dressing and the 2 teaspoons fresh or ½ teaspoon dried rosemary; brush over vegetables.

Grill kabobs on the rack of an uncovered grill directly over medium heat for 10 to 12 minutes or until vegetables are tender and browned, turning and brushing occasionally with dressing mixture. If desired, garnish with additional fresh rosemary.

Nutrition facts per serving: 161 cal., 8 g total fat (1 g sat. fat), 0 mg chol., 217 mg sodium, 22 g carbo., 2 g fiber, 3 g pro. Daily values: 15% vit. A, 75% vit. C, 2% calcium, 7% iron

*Note: Using rosemary skewers will add a special touch to your meal. To use fresh rosemary skewers, first grill the vegetables on regular metal skewers (the rosemary will burn if grilled), then thread grilled vegetables on long stalks of fresh rosemary, removing some of the rosemary leaves.

8  tiny new potatoes, quartered

2  tablespoons water

8  baby sunburst squash

4  miniature sweet peppers and/or 1 red sweet pepper, cut into 1-inch pieces

8  tiny red onions, halved, or 2 small red onions, each cut into 8 wedges

8  baby zucchini or 1 small zucchini, halved lengthwise and sliced

¼  cup bottled oil-and-vinegar salad dressing

2  teaspoons snipped fresh rosemary or ½ teaspoon dried rosemary, crushed

**Fresh rosemary (optional)**

# eggplant with gorgonzola

The mild, sweet taste and meaty texture of eggplant lends itself especially well to grilling. This lovely combination of glossy purple eggplant, yellow summer squash, and red onion is the perfect accompaniment to grilled chicken.

74

1 small eggplant (about 12 ounces)

1 medium yellow summer squash, halved lengthwise and sliced 1 inch thick

1 small red onion, cut into thin wedges

2 tablespoons pesto

¼ cup crumbled Gorgonzola or other blue cheese, feta cheese, or goat (chèvre) cheese (1 ounce)

**Prep: 10 minutes    Grill: 20 minutes**
**Makes 4 servings**

If desired, peel eggplant. Cut into 1-inch cubes. In a large bowl combine the eggplant, squash, onion, and pesto; toss gently to coat. Fold a 36×18-inch piece of heavy foil in half to make an 18×18-inch square. Place vegetables in center of foil. Bring up 2 opposite edges of foil; seal with a double fold. Fold the remaining ends to completely enclose the vegetables, leaving space for steam to build.*

Grill vegetables on the rack of an uncovered grill directly over medium heat for 20 to 25 minutes or until vegetables are crisp-tender, turning them occasionally.

To serve, transfer vegetables to a serving bowl and sprinkle with cheese.

Nutrition facts per serving: 116 cal., 8 g total fat (2 g sat. fat), 7 mg chol., 179 mg sodium, 9 g carbo., 3 g fiber, 4 g pro. Daily values: 3% vit. A, 5% vit. C, 4% calcium, 2% iron

*Note: If desired, you may assemble the foil packet ahead of time and refrigerate until ready to grill. Add a few minutes to the grilling time.

# peppers stuffed with goat cheese

Stuffed peppers just got lighter and more elegant! These easy-to-make sweet peppers filled with creamy, tangy goat cheese and loads of fresh herbs make impressive, yet quick, company fare that will complement a grilled steak and a hearty glass of wine.

**Prep: 15 minutes    Grill: 5 minutes**
**Makes 4 servings**

In a medium covered saucepan cook peppers in a small amount of boiling water for 2 minutes. Drain, cut sides down, on paper towels.

Meanwhile, for cheese mixture, in a small bowl combine goat cheese, Monterey Jack cheese, chives, and basil. Spoon into pepper shells.

Fold a 24×18-inch piece of heavy foil in half to make a 12×18-inch rectangle. Place peppers in center of foil. Bring up 2 opposite edges of foil; seal with a double fold. Fold remaining ends to completely enclose peppers, leaving space for steam to build.

Grill peppers on the rack of an uncovered grill directly over medium to medium-hot heat for 5 to 6 minutes or until peppers are crisp-tender and cheese is melted.

Nutrition facts per serving: 60 cal., 4 g total fat (2 g sat. fat), 13 mg chol., 80 mg sodium, 3 g carbo., 0 g fiber, 3 g pro. Daily values: 30% vit. A, 104% vit. C, 4% calcium

- 2 medium red, yellow, or green sweet peppers, halved lengthwise
- 1 ounce soft goat (chèvre) cheese
- ¼ cup shredded Monterey Jack cheese (1 ounce)
- 1 tablespoon snipped fresh chives
- 1 tablespoon snipped fresh basil or 1 teaspoon dried basil, crushed

# grilled tomatoes with pesto

They say there are two things money can't buy: love and homegrown tomatoes. If you don't have the latter, search out a farmer's market for the makings of this summer dish. It will garner you love from all who are lucky enough to taste it.

**Prep: 15 minutes   Grill: 15 minutes**
**Makes 6 servings**

Using a spoon, hollow out the top ¼ inch of tomato halves. Top with pesto, then onion slices. Place tomatoes in a foil pie plate.

In a grill with a cover arrange preheated coals around edge of grill. Test for medium heat in center of the grill. Place the tomatoes in center of grill rack. Cover and grill for 10 to 15 minutes or until tomatoes are heated through.

Meanwhile, in a small bowl stir together cheese, almonds, and parsley. Sprinkle over tomatoes. Cover and grill about 5 minutes more or until cheese is melted. Sprinkle lightly with salt and pepper.

Nutrition facts per serving: 132 cal., 10 g total fat (2 g sat. fat), 9 mg chol., 119 mg sodium, 6 g carbo., 2 g fiber, 5 g pro. Daily values: 7% vit. A, 24% vit. C, 8% calcium, 5% iron

- 3 **to 5 small to medium red, orange, and/or yellow tomatoes, cored and halved crosswise**
- 2 **tablespoons pesto**
- 6 **very thin onion slices**
- ½ **cup shredded Monterey Jack cheese (2 ounces)**
- ⅓ **cup smoky-flavored whole almonds, chopped**
- 2 **tablespoons snipped fresh parsley**

# summer squash
## with cheese & sage

The smaller the squash you choose, the sweeter they are likely to be. As the squash cook, their natural sugar caramelizes—giving them a nutty, rich flavor. They soak up a wonderful, smoky flavor, too—a terrific combination with the salty tang of goat cheese.

78

- 1 **pound small yellow summer squash or zucchini**
- 1 **teaspoon olive oil**
- ¼ **cup mild picante sauce**
- 2 **tablespoons crumbled goat (chèvre) cheese or shredded Monterey Jack cheese**
- 1 **tablespoon snipped fresh sage, oregano, or cilantro**

**Prep: 5 minutes   Grill: 10 minutes**
**Makes 4 servings**

Trim ends from squash; halve squash lengthwise. In a medium bowl combine squash and oil; toss gently to coat.

Grill squash, cut sides down, on the greased rack of an uncovered grill directly over medium heat about 10 minutes or until squash are crisp-tender, turning once and brushing occasionally with picante sauce. Transfer squash to a serving bowl and sprinkle with cheese and sage.

Nutrition facts per serving: 54 cal., 4 g total fat (1 g sat. fat), 7 mg chol., 156 mg sodium, 5 g carbo., 1 g fiber, 2 g pro. Daily values: 4% vit. A, 14% vit. C, 1% calcium, 3% iron

## fresh-herb interchanges
Fresh herbs turn ordinary dishes into extraordinary ones. Herbs each have their own distinct flavors, but you can have one step in for another. Try these substitutions:
- **Sage:** use savory, marjoram, or rosemary
- **Basil:** substitute oregano or thyme
- **Thyme:** basil, marjoram, oregano, or savory will suffice
- **Mint:** substitute basil, marjoram, or rosemary
- **Rosemary:** try thyme, tarragon, or savory
- **Cilantro:** substitute parsley

# summer squash combo

This humble squash gets a French accent with deeply flavored walnut oil—a Gallic favorite. Walnut oil is delicate and should be refrigerated. If the oil becomes cloudy and solid, let it stand several minutes at room temperature before using.

**Prep: 15 minutes   Grill: 5 minutes**
**Makes 4 to 6 servings**

In a small bowl stir together walnut oil, the 1 tablespoon olive oil, the rosemary, salt, red pepper, and garlic. Brush the onions, zucchini, and yellow squash with some of the oil mixture.

Grill vegetables on the rack of an uncovered grill directly over medium to medium-hot heat for 5 to 6 minutes or until crisp-tender and lightly browned, turning and brushing once with remaining oil mixture.

Nutrition facts per serving: 126 cal., 10 g total fat (1 g sat. fat), 0 mg chol., 272 mg sodium, 8 g carbo., 2 g fiber, 1 g pro. Daily values: 4% vit. A, 12% vit. C, 2% calcium, 3% iron

2 tablespoons walnut oil or olive oil

1 tablespoon olive oil

2 teaspoons snipped fresh rosemary or ½ teaspoon dried rosemary, crushed

½ teaspoon salt

½ to 1 teaspoon crushed red pepper

½ teaspoon bottled minced garlic

2 medium red onions, cut crosswise into ¾-inch-thick slices

2 medium zucchini, cut lengthwise into quarters

2 medium yellow summer squash, cut lengthwise into quarters

# warm tarragon potato salad

A picnic favorite has been lightened and brightened up with a tangy fresh-herb and Dijon vinaigrette dressing, crunchy bok choy, and peppery radishes. Tarragon, with its aniselike flavor, makes a fine complement to mild foods such as potatoes or fish.

80

¼ cup salad oil

¼ cup vinegar

1 tablespoon sugar (optional)

1 teaspoon snipped fresh tarragon or dill or ¼ teaspoon dried tarragon, crushed, or dried dillweed

½ teaspoon Dijon-style mustard

1 pound tiny new potatoes and/or small yellow potatoes, cut into bite-size pieces

2 teaspoons salad oil

1 cup chopped bok choy

½ cup chopped red radishes

½ cup thinly sliced green onions

2 thin slices Canadian-style bacon, chopped (1 ounce)

⅛ teaspoon freshly ground pepper

4 artichokes, cooked, halved lengthwise, and choke removed (optional)

**Prep: 10 minutes   Grill: 25 minutes**
**Makes 8 servings**

For dressing, in a small bowl whisk together the ¼ cup oil, the vinegar, sugar (if desired), tarragon, and mustard. Set aside.

In a lightly greased 2-quart square foil pan combine potatoes and the 2 teaspoons oil; toss to coat.

In a grill with a cover arrange preheated coals around edge of grill. Test for medium-hot heat in center of grill. Place potatoes in center of grill rack. Cover and grill about 25 minutes or just until potatoes are tender. Cool potatoes slightly.

In a large bowl combine potatoes, bok choy, radishes, green onions, Canadian-style bacon, and pepper. Add the dressing; toss gently to coat. If desired, spoon the salad into artichoke halves.

Nutrition facts per serving: 135 cal., 8 g total fat (1 g sat. fat), 2 mg chol., 68 mg sodium, 14 g carbo., 1 g fiber, 2 g pro. Daily values: 2% vit. A, 21% vit. C, 2% calcium, 7% iron

# grilled asparagus with sorrel dressing

The essence of lemon brings out the very best in fresh asparagus. Here, the lemony tartness comes from delicate sorrel greens, which are used to flavor the fresh-tasting yogurt-mayonnaise dressing. Look for sorrel especially in the spring.

¼ **cup plain low-fat yogurt**

¼ **cup mayonnaise or salad dressing**

¼ **cup finely snipped sorrel or spinach**

1 **green onion, thinly sliced**

1 **teaspoon lemon-pepper seasoning (optional)**

1 **pound asparagus spears**

2 **tablespoons water**

**Prep: 10 minutes   Grill: 15 minutes**
**Makes 4 servings**

For dressing, in a small bowl combine yogurt, mayonnaise, sorrel, green onion, and, if desired, lemon-pepper seasoning. Cover and refrigerate until ready to serve.

Fold a 36×18-inch piece of heavy foil in half to make an 18×18-inch square. Snap off and discard the woody bases from asparagus. Place asparagus in center of foil. Fold up edges of foil slightly; drizzle asparagus with water. Bring up 2 opposite edges of foil; seal with a double fold. Fold remaining ends to completely enclose the asparagus, leaving space for steam to build.

Grill asparagus on the rack of an uncovered grill directly over medium-hot heat about 15 minutes or until crisp-tender, turning once. Serve asparagus with the dressing.

Nutrition facts per serving: 129 cal., 11 g total fat (2 g sat. fat), 9 mg chol., 95 mg sodium, 5 g carbo., 2 g fiber, 3 g pro. Daily values: 10% vit. A, 38% vit. C, 4% calcium, 5% iron

# cilantro corn on the cob

The pleasures of the American summer could be distilled into this: tender, sweet corn on the cob, roasted and bursting with fresh herb flavor. Try substituting fresh basil for the cilantro, if you like—and pass the napkins, please.

**Prep: 10 minutes  Grill: 20 minutes**
**Makes 4 servings**

In a bowl combine cilantro, oil, red pepper, salt, and black pepper. Remove husks from corn. Scrub ears with a stiff brush to remove silks. Rinse corn; pat dry. Place each ear of corn on a piece of heavy foil. Brush ears with cilantro mixture. Wrap the corn securely in foil. Grill corn on the rack of an uncovered grill directly over medium to medium-hot heat about 20 minutes or until kernels are tender, turning frequently.

Nutrition facts per serving: 116 cal., 4 g total fat (1 g sat. fat), 0 mg chol., 90 mg sodium, 20 g carbo., 3 g fiber, 3 g pro. Daily values: 8% vit. A, 7% vit. C, 4% iron

- 1  tablespoon snipped fresh cilantro
- 1  tablespoon olive oil
- 1  to 2 teaspoons crushed red pepper
- ⅛  teaspoon salt
-    Dash black pepper
- 4  fresh ears of corn

## it's hot, hot, hot (or not)

Unless you have a thermometer on your grill, you'll need a good way to measure the approximate temperature of the coals. Here's a simple test: Hold your hand where the food will cook for as long as it's comfortable. The number of seconds you can hold it there gives you a clue.

| Number of Seconds | Coal Temperature |
| --- | --- |
| 2 | High |
| 3 | Medium-high |
| 4 | Medium |
| 5 | Medium-low |
| 6 | Low |

# sauces, marinades, & rubs

# herb rub

Here's an aromatic way to flavor grilled meats that doesn't depend on having fresh herbs. Try this rub on steak or chicken.

**Prep: 5 minutes**
**Makes about 2 teaspoons, enough for 2½ to 3 pounds bone-in chicken (6 servings).**

In a small bowl combine ½ teaspoon salt; ½ teaspoon dried thyme, crushed; ½ teaspoon dried rosemary, crushed; ½ teaspoon dried savory, crushed; and ¼ teaspoon pepper. Sprinkle the mixture evenly over chicken; rub in with your fingers.

Grill chicken according to charts on pages 90 to 93.

Nutrition facts per serving (using chicken pieces): 113 cal., 2 g total fat (1 g sat. fat), 50 mg chol., 312 mg sodium, 0 g carbo., 0 g fiber, 21 g pro. Daily values: 1% calcium, 7% iron

# herbed pecan rub

Give a Southern accent to chicken or fish. The ground pecans toast and turn golden as they cook, forming a sweet, savory crust.

**Prep: 15 minutes**
**Makes about ½ cup, enough for 3 pounds fish fillets or boneless chicken (12 servings).**

In a blender container or food processor bowl combine ½ cup broken pecans; ½ cup fresh oregano leaves; ½ cup fresh thyme leaves; 3 cloves garlic, cut up; ½ teaspoon pepper; ½ teaspoon finely shredded lemon peel; and ¼ teaspoon salt. Cover; blend or process with several on-off turns until a paste forms, stopping several times and scraping the sides.

With the machine running, gradually add ¼ cup cooking oil until mixture forms a paste. Rub onto fish or chicken. Grill fish or chicken, using indirect heat, according to charts on pages 90 to 93.

Nutrition facts per serving (using fish fillets): 175 cal., 9 g total fat (1 g sat. fat), 60 mg chol., 137 mg sodium, 1 g carbo., 0 g fiber, 22 g pro. Daily values: 1% vit. A, 2% calcium, 2% iron

## apple butter
## barbecue sauce

Apple butter—an old-fashioned favorite for spreading on bread—is the base for this very simple sauce. Try it with chicken or pork.

**Prep: 8 minutes**
**Makes about 1⅓ cups, enough for 1 to 2 pounds boneless poultry or pork (4 to 8 servings).**

In a small saucepan combine one 8-ounce can tomato sauce, ½ cup apple butter, and 1 tablespoon Pickapeppa sauce or Worcestershire sauce. Bring just to boiling; remove from heat.

Grill poultry or pork according to charts on pages 90 to 93, brushing occasionally with sauce the last 10 minutes of grilling. Heat any remaining sauce just until bubbly, stirring occasionally. Serve sauce with poultry or pork.

Nutrition facts per serving (using skinless, boneless chicken): 215 cal., 4 g total fat (1 g sat. fat), 59 mg chol., 432 mg sodium, 22 g carbo., 1 g fiber, 22 g pro. Daily values: 6% vit. A, 15% vit. C, 2% calcium, 10% iron

## honey-peach sauce

This sweet sauce is the taste of summer boiled down to the basics: juicy peaches, honey, zingy cracked black pepper, and fresh thyme.

**Prep: 25 minutes**
**Makes about 1¾ cups, enough for 2 to 3 pounds boneless pork or beef (8 to 12 servings).**

Peel and cut up 3 medium peaches. Place in a blender container. Add 2 tablespoons lemon juice, 2 tablespoons honey, and ½ teaspoon cracked pepper. Cover and blend until smooth. Transfer to a saucepan. Bring to boiling; reduce heat. Simmer, uncovered, about 15 minutes or until slightly thickened, stirring occasionally. Peel and finely chop 1 medium peach; stir into the sauce. Stir in 1 to 2 teaspoons snipped fresh thyme.

Grill meat according to charts on pages 90 to 93, brushing with sauce the last 15 minutes of grilling. Heat remaining sauce until bubbly. Serve with meat.

Nutrition facts per serving (using boneless pork loin chops): 189 cal., 7 g total fat (3 g sat. fat), 51 mg chol., 39 mg sodium, 14 g carbo., 1 g fiber, 17 g pro. Daily values: 40% vit. A, 12% vit. C, 5% iron

# five-alarm sauce

If you can't get to Kansas City, Houston, or some other smoke-and-fire hub, turn your backyard into BBQ central with this multispiced sauce.

**Prep: 15 minutes   Cook: 5 minutes**
**Makes 2½ cups, enough for 2 to 3 pounds boneless beef or poultry (12 servings).**

In a small saucepan stir together 1 cup catsup; 1 large tomato, peeled, seeded, and chopped; 1 small green pepper, chopped; 2 tablespoons chopped onion; 2 tablespoons brown sugar; 1 to 2 tablespoons steak sauce; 1 to 2 tablespoons Worcestershire sauce; ½ teaspoon garlic powder; ¼ teaspoon each ground nutmeg, ground cinnamon, and ground cloves; and ⅛ teaspoon each ground ginger and pepper. Bring to boiling; reduce heat. Cover; simmer about 5 minutes or until green pepper is crisp-tender. Grill beef or poultry according to charts on pages 90 to 93. Serve sauce with beef or chicken.

Nutrition facts per serving (using beef brisket): 173 cal., 7 g total fat (3 g sat. fat), 52 mg chol., 347 mg sodium, 10 g carbo., 1 g fiber, 17 g pro. Daily values: 3% vit. A, 19% vit. C, 1% calcium, 12% iron

# peanut saté sauce

When the mood strikes for something slightly exotic, stir up this rich saté sauce with Thai overtones. It's particularly fitting with chicken.

**Prep: 10 minutes**
**Makes about ½ cup sauce, enough for 2 pounds boneless meat (8 servings).**

In a small bowl stir together ¼ cup creamy peanut butter, 2 tablespoons rice vinegar or white vinegar, 2 tablespoons soy sauce, 1 teaspoon minced garlic, ½ teaspoon toasted sesame oil, and ⅛ teaspoon crushed red pepper. Stir in 2 tablespoons thinly sliced green onion.

Grill meat according to charts on pages 90 to 93, brushing occasionally with sauce the last 5 minutes of grilling. Heat any remaining sauce until bubbly, stirring occasionally. Serve with meat.

Nutrition facts per serving (using pork top loin chops): 235 cal., 16 g total fat (4 g sat. fat), 51 mg chol., 373 mg sodium, 4 g carbo., 1 g fiber, 20 g pro. Daily values: 1% vit. C, 6% iron

# garlic-basil marinade

If you choose the fresh herb option, grill the meat or poultry indirectly (see tip box, page 42). Otherwise, the herbs will burn.

**Prep: 10 minutes**
**Makes about 1 cup, enough for 2 to 2½ pounds bone-in chicken (6 servings).**

Rinse chicken; pat dry. Place chicken in a plastic bag set in a shallow dish. For marinade, combine ⅔ cup dry white wine or white wine vinegar; ⅓ cup olive oil or cooking oil; 1 thinly sliced green onion; 2 tablespoons snipped fresh basil or 2 teaspoons dried basil, crushed; 1 teaspoon sugar; and 1 teaspoon minced garlic. Pour over chicken; close bag. Marinate in refrigerator for 6 to 24 hours, turning bag occasionally. Drain chicken, reserving marinade. Grill chicken according to charts on pages 90 to 93, brushing with marinade up to the last 5 minutes of grilling. Discard any remaining marinade.

Nutrition facts per serving (using meaty chicken pieces): 235 cal., 14 g total fat (3 g sat. fat), 69 mg chol., 62 mg sodium, 1 g carbo., 0 g fiber, 22 g pro. Daily values: 2% vit. A, 1% calcium, 6% iron

# herb-dijon marinade

Robust mustard and the distinctive flavor of lamb make ideal partners. The combination of herbs adds a pleasant taste twist. Also try it on beef.

**Prep: 10 minutes**
**Makes about 1⅓ cups, enough for 5 to 6 pounds bone-in lamb or beef (12 to 14 servings).**

Place meat in a shallow dish. Combine one 8-ounce jar (¾ cup) Dijon-style mustard; ⅓ cup dry white wine; ¼ cup cooking oil; 1 teaspoon dried rosemary, crushed; 1 teaspoon dried basil, crushed; 1 teaspoon minced garlic; ½ teaspoon dried oregano, crushed; ½ teaspoon dried thyme, crushed; and ¼ teaspoon pepper. Spread over meat. Cover; marinate at room temperature 1 hour or in refrigerator 2 to 24 hours.

Drain meat, reserving marinade. Cover; refrigerate marinade until ready to serve. Grill meat according to charts on pages 90 to 93. Heat marinade until bubbly, stirring occasionally. Serve with meat.

Nutrition facts per serving (using leg of lamb): 240 cal., 13 g total fat (3 g sat. fat), 77 mg chol., 536 mg sodium, 2 g carbo., 0 g fiber, 25 g pro. Daily values: 1% calcium, 13% iron

# ginger-rum marinade

Get a taste of the tropics in every bite of beef, pork, or chicken with this terrific island-inspired, pineapple-flavored marinade.

**Prep: 5 minutes**
**Makes about 1¼ cups, enough for 2 pounds boneless meat (8 servings).**

Place meat in a plastic bag set in a shallow dish. For marinade, combine ½ cup unsweetened pineapple juice, ⅓ cup rum, ¼ cup soy sauce, 1 tablespoon brown sugar, 1 tablespoon grated gingerroot, 1 teaspoon bottled minced garlic, and ¼ teaspoon ground red pepper. Pour over meat; close bag. Marinate in refrigerator for 4 to 8 hours, turning the bag occasionally.

Drain meat, reserving marinade. Grill the meat according to the charts on pages 90 to 93, brushing occasionally with marinade up to the last 5 minutes. Discard any remaining marinade.

Nutrition facts per serving (using boneless beef sirloin steaks): 215 cal., 10 g total fat (4 g sat. fat), 76 mg chol., 228 mg sodium, 2 g carbo., 0 g fiber, 26 g pro. Daily values: 1% vit. C, 19% iron

# lemon-rosemary marinade

Rosemary, an herb with an assertive flavor, adds interest to this refreshing lemon marinade for fish, seafood, or chicken.

**Prep: 8 minutes**
**Makes about ¾ cup, enough for 1 to 1½ pounds fish fillets or boneless poultry (4 to 6 servings).**

Rinse fish; pat dry. Place in a plastic bag set in a shallow dish. Combine 1 teaspoon finely shredded lemon peel; ⅓ cup lemon juice; ¼ cup olive oil or cooking oil; ¼ cup white wine Worcestershire sauce; 1 tablespoon sugar; 1 tablespoon snipped fresh rosemary or 1 teaspoon dried rosemary, crushed; ¼ teaspoon salt; and ⅛ teaspoon pepper. Pour over fish; close bag. Marinate in refrigerator for 1 to 2 hours, turning bag occasionally. Drain, reserving marinade. Grill fish according to charts on pages 90 to 93, brushing with marinade up to the last 5 minutes. Discard any remaining marinade.

Nutrition facts per serving (using fish fillets): 151 cal., 6 g total fat (1 g sat. fat), 60 mg chol., 179 mg sodium, 3 g carbo., 0 g fiber, 21 g pro. Daily values: 1% vit. A, 6% vit. C, 1% calcium, 2% iron

## poultry

If desired, remove the skin from the poultry. Rinse poultry and pat dry with paper towels. Test for desired coal temperature (see tip, page 83). Place poultry on the grill rack, bone side up, directly over the preheated coals (for direct grilling) or directly over drip pan (for indirect grilling). Grill (uncovered for direct grilling or covered for indirect grilling) for the time given below or until tender and no longer pink. (Note: White meat will cook slightly faster.) Turn poultry over halfway through the grilling time.

| Type of Bird | Weight | Temperature | Doneness | Direct Grilling* Time | Indirect Grilling* Time |
| --- | --- | --- | --- | --- | --- |
| Chicken, broiler-fryer, half | 1¼ to 1½ pounds | Medium | Tender; no longer pink | 40 to 50 minutes | 1 to 1¼ hours |
| Chicken breast half, skinned and boned | 4 to 5 ounces each | Medium | Tender; no longer pink | 12 to 15 minute | 15 to 18 minutes |
| Chicken quarters | 2½ to 3 pounds total | Medium | Tender; no longer pink | 40 to 50 minutes | 50 to 60 minutes |
| Meaty chicken pieces | 2 to 2½ pounds total | Medium | Tender; no longer pink | 35 to 45 minutes | 50 to 60 minutes |
| Turkey breast tenderloin steak | 4 to 6 ounces each | Medium | Tender; no longer pink | 12 to 15 minutes | 15 to 18 minutes |

*Note: Most recipes in this book are grilled by direct heat unless otherwise noted. For differences in methods, see tip, page 42.

# beef, pork, or lamb

Test for the desired temperature (see tip, page 83). Place the meat on the rack of a grill directly over the preheated coals (for direct grilling) or directly over a drip pan (for indirect grilling). Grill meat (uncovered for direct grilling or covered for indirect grilling) for the time given below or until done, turning the meat over halfway through the grilling time.

| Cut | Thickness | Temperature | Doneness | Direct Grilling* Time | Indirect Grilling* Time |
|---|---|---|---|---|---|
| **Beef** | | | | | |
| Boneless sirloin steak | 1 inch | Medium | Medium rare | 14 to 18 minutes | 22 to 26 minutes |
| | | | Medium | 18 to 22 minutes | 26 to 30 minutes |
| | 1½ inches | Medium | Medium rare | 32 to 36 minutes | 32 to 36 minutes |
| | | | Medium | 36 to 40 minutes | 36 to 40 minutes |
| Flank steak | ¾ to 1 inch | Medium | Medium | 12 to 14 minutes | 18 to 22 minutes |
| Ground meat patties | ¾ inch (4 per pound) | Medium | No pink remains | 14 to 18 minutes | 20 to 24 minutes |
| Steak (blade, chuck, top round) | 1 inch | Medium | Medium rare | 14 to 16 minutes | 45 to 55 minutes |
| | | | Medium | 18 to 20 minutes | 60 to 70 minutes |
| | 1½ inches | Medium | Medium rare | 19 to 26 minutes | 50 to 60 minutes |
| | | | Medium | 27 to 32 minutes | 1 to 1¼ hours |
| Steak (porterhouse, rib, rib eye, sirloin, T-bone, tenderloin, top loin) | 1 inch | Medium | Medium rare | 8 to 12 minutes | 16 to 20 minutes |
| | | | Medium | 12 to 15 minutes | 20 to 24 minutes |
| | 1¼ to 1½ inches | Medium | Medium rare | 14 to 18 minutes | 20 to 22 minutes |
| | | | Medium | 18 to 22 minutes | 22 to 26 minutes |
| **Pork**\*\* | | | | | |
| Chop | ¾ inch | Medium | Medium | 8 to 11 minutes | 20 to 24 minutes |
| | 1¼ to 1½ inches | Medium | Medium | 25 to 30 minutes | 35 to 40 minutes |
| **Lamb** | | | | | |
| Chop | 1 inch | Medium | Medium rare | 10 to 14 minutes | 16 to 18 minutes |
| | | Medium | 14 to 16 minutes | 18 to 20 minutes | |
| **Kabobs** | 1-inch cubes | Medium | Medium | 12 to 14 minutes | |

*Note: Most recipes in this book are grilled by direct heat unless otherwise noted. For differences in methods, see tip page 42.
\*\*Note: Pork should be cooked until juices run clear.

## fish & seafood

Thaw fish or shellfish, if frozen. Test for desired temperature (see tip, page 83). For fish fillets, place in a well-greased grill basket. For fish steaks and whole fish, grease the grill rack. Place the fish on the rack directly over the preheated coals (for direct grilling) or over a drip pan (for indirect grilling). Grill (uncovered for direct grilling or covered for indirect grilling), for the time given below or until the fish just begins to flake easily when tested with a fork; scallops and shrimp should look opaque. Turn the fish over halfway through the grilling time. If desired, brush fish with melted margarine or butter.

| Form of Fish | Weight, Size, or Thickness | Temperature | Doneness | Direct Grilling* Time | Indirect Grilling Time |
|---|---|---|---|---|---|
| **Dressed fish** | ½ to 1½ pounds | Medium | Flakes | 7 to 9 minutes per ½ pound | 20 to 25 minutes per ½ pound |
| **Fillets, steaks, cubes** (for kabobs) | ½ to 1 inch thick | Medium | Flakes | 4 to 6 minutes per ½-inch thickness | 4 to 6 minutes per ½-inch thickness |
| **Sea scallops** (for kabobs) | (12 to 15 per pound) | Medium | Opaque | 5 to 8 minutes | 5 to 7 minutes |
| **Shrimp** (for kabobs) | Medium (20 per pound) | Medium | Opaque | 6 to 8 minutes | 6 to 8 minutes |
| | Jumbo (12 to 15 per pound) | Medium | Opaque | 10 to 12 minutes | 8 to 10 minutes |

*Note: Most recipes in this book are grilled by direct heat unless otherwise noted. For differences in methods, see tip page 42.

# vegetables

Before grilling, rinse, trim, cut up, and precook vegetables as directed below. To precook vegetables, in a saucepan bring a small amount of water to boiling; add desired vegetable and simmer, covered, for the time specified in the chart. Drain well. Generously brush vegetables with olive oil, margarine, or butter before grilling to prevent vegetables from sticking to the grill rack. Test for desired temperature (see tip, page 83).

To grill, place vegetables on a piece of heavy foil or on the grill rack directly over the preheated coals. If putting vegetables directly on grill rack, lay them perpendicular to wires of the rack so they won't fall into the coals. Grill, uncovered, for the time given below or until tender, turning occasionally. Monitor the grilling closely so vegetables don't char.

| Vegetable | Preparation | Precooking Time | Direct-Grilling* Time |
|-----------|-------------|-----------------|------------------------|
| Asparagus | Snap off and discard tough bases of stems. Precook, then tie asparagus in bundles with strips of cooked green onion tops. | 3 to 4 minutes | 3 to 5 minutes |
| Corn on the cob | Remove husks from corn. Scrub ears with a stiff brush to remove silks. Rinse corn; pat dry. | Do not precook | 20 to 30 minutes |
| Eggplant | Cut off top and blossom ends. Cut eggplant crosswise into 1-inch-thick slices. | Do not precook | 8 minutes |
| Fennel | Snip off feathery leaves. Cut off stems. | 10 minutes, then cut into 6 to 8 wedges | 8 minutes |
| Fresh baby carrots | Cut off carrot tops. Wash and peel carrots. | 3 to 5 minutes | 3 to 5 minutes |
| Leeks | Cut off green tops; trim bulb roots and remove 1 or 2 layers of white skin. | 10 minutes or until tender; then halve lengthwise | 5 minutes |
| New potatoes | Halve potatoes. | 10 minutes or until almost tender | 10 to 12 minutes |
| Pattypan squash | Rinse; trim ends. | 3 minutes | 20 minutes |
| Sweet peppers | Remove stems. Quarter peppers. Remove seeds and membranes. Cut into 1-inch-wide strips. | Do not precook | 8 to 10 minutes |
| Zucchini or yellow summer squash | Wash; cut off ends. Quarter lengthwise. | Do not precook | 5 to 6 minutes |

*Note: Because vegetables contain little fat to drip off, they don't require a drip pan. Therefore, timings are given for direct grilling only.

**94**

By making a few conversions, cooks in Australia, Canada, and the United Kingdom can use the recipes in Better Homes and Gardens® *Fresh and Simple™ 5 O'Clock Grill* with confidence. The charts on this page provide a guide for converting measurements from the U.S. customary system, which is used throughout this book, to the imperial and metric systems. There also is a conversion table for oven temperatures to accommodate the differences in oven calibrations.

**Product Differences:** Most of the ingredients called for in the recipes in this book are available in English-speaking countries. However, some are known by different names. Here are some common American ingredients and their possible counterparts:

- Sugar is granulated or castor sugar.
- Powdered sugar is icing sugar.
- All-purpose flour is plain household flour or white flour. When self-rising flour is used in place of all-purpose flour in a recipe that calls for leavening, omit the leavening agent (baking soda or baking powder) and salt.
- Light corn syrup is golden syrup.
- Cornstarch is cornflour.
- Baking soda is bicarbonate of soda.
- Vanilla is vanilla essence.
- Green, red, or yellow sweet peppers are capsicums.
- Sultanas are golden raisins.

**Volume and Weight:** Americans traditionally use cup measures for liquid and solid ingredients. The chart, above right, shows the approximate imperial and metric equivalents. If you are accustomed to weighing solid ingredients, the following approximate equivalents will be helpful.

- 1 cup butter, castor sugar, or rice = 8 ounces = about 250 grams
- 1 cup flour = 4 ounces = about 125 grams
- 1 cup icing sugar = 5 ounces = about 150 grams

Spoon measures are used for smaller amounts of ingredients. Although the size of the tablespoon varies slightly in different countries, for practical purposes and for recipes in this book, a straight substitution is all that's necessary.

Measurements made using cups or spoons always should be level unless stated otherwise.

## Equivalents: U.S. = Australia/U.K.

⅛ teaspoon = 0.5 ml
¼ teaspoon = 1 ml
½ teaspoon = 2 ml
1 teaspoon = 5 ml
1 tablespoon = 1 tablespoon
¼ cup = 2 tablespoons = 2 fluid ounces = 60 ml
⅓ cup = ¼ cup = 3 fluid ounces = 90 ml
½ cup = ⅓ cup = 4 fluid ounces = 120 ml
⅔ cup = ½ cup = 5 fluid ounces = 150 ml
¾ cup = ⅔ cup = 6 fluid ounces = 180 ml
1 cup = ¾ cup = 8 fluid ounces = 240 ml
1¼ cups = 1 cup
2 cups = 1 pint
1 quart = 1 liter
½ inch =1.27 cm
1 inch = 2.54 cm

## Baking Pan Sizes

| American | Metric |
|---|---|
| 8×1½-inch round baking pan | 20×4-cm cake tin |
| 9×1½-inch round baking pan | 23×3.5-cm cake tin |
| 11×7×1½-inch baking pan | 28×18×4-cm baking tin |
| 13×9×2-inch baking pan | 30×20×3-cm baking tin |
| 2-quart rectangular baking dish | 30×20×3-cm baking tin |
| 15×10×1-inch baking pan | 30×25×2-cm baking tin (Swiss roll tin) |
| 9-inch pie plate | 22×4- or 23×4-cm pie plate |
| 7- or 8-inch springform pan | 18- or 20-cm springform or loose-bottom cake tin |
| 9×5×3-inch loaf pan | 23×13×7-cm or 2-pound narrow loaf tin or pâté tin |
| 1½-quart casserole | 1.5-liter casserole |
| 2-quart casserole | 2-liter casserole |

## Oven Temperature Equivalents

| Fahrenheit Setting | Celsius Setting* | Gas Setting |
|---|---|---|
| 300°F | 150°C | Gas Mark 2 (slow) |
| 325°F | 160°C | Gas Mark 3 (moderately slow) |
| 350°F | 180°C | Gas Mark 4 (moderate) |
| 375°F | 190°C | Gas Mark 5 (moderately hot) |
| 400°F | 200°C | Gas Mark 6 (hot) |
| 425°F | 220°C | Gas Mark 7 |
| 450°F | 230°C | Gas Mark 8 (very hot) |
| Broil | | Grill |

*\* Electric and gas ovens may be calibrated using Celsius. However, for an electric oven, increase the Celsius setting 10 to 20 degrees when cooking above 160°C. For convection or forced-air ovens (gas or electric), lower the temperature setting 10°C when cooking at all heat levels.*